JANE'S WORLD

A Memoir in Stories & Poems

JANE'S WORLD

A Memoir in Stories & Poems

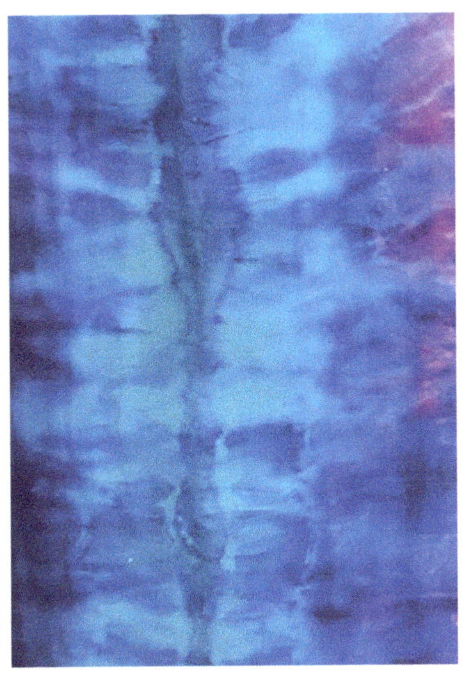

Jane Watkins

Edited by Martha Fuller

Layout and design by Sharon E Rawlins

Cover Image: tie-dye fabric by Jane Watkins

Artwork Illustrations: drawings, paintings, ceramics, batik, tie-dye, and jewelry by Jane Watkins

Author Photograph by Kate Arnesen

Aloha Jane Press

alohajanepress@gmail.com

ISBN 979-8-218-84333-5 Paperback
ISBN 979-8-218-84334-2 eBook

Printed in the United States of America

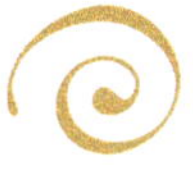

To my beloved daughter Lea
& grandson Ronan

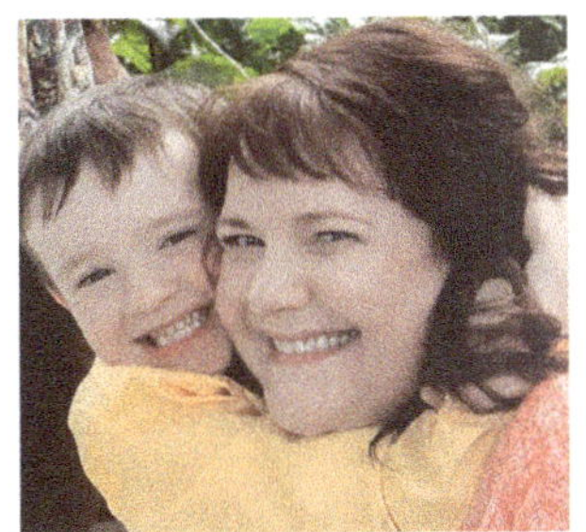

CONTENTS

Stories

CONTENTS

Poems

Dearly Departed

Infinite Light

Hawaii—The Big Island

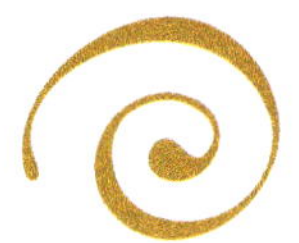

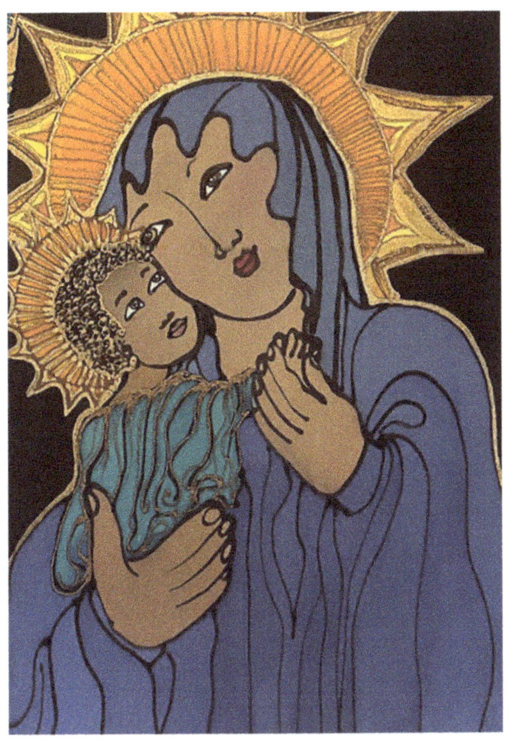

God's Mother

God's mother knows everything—how he was born,
when he was naughty and misbehaved.

She loves every corner of space, every single breath,
everyone, everything, every time.

She takes down the stars with her fingertips,
puts them on as earrings.

She is the reason we came out learning,
yearning to return to her.

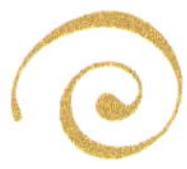

Moving To Lebanon—My Paradise

1951

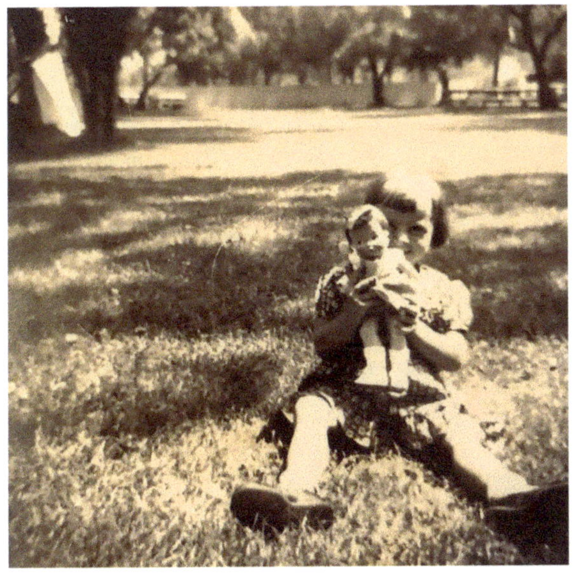

Me age 4

My mother was twenty-five when she made the journey from California, via New York City and Paris, to join my father in Lebanon. A year and half earlier, he had taken a job running a pump station for the Saudi Arabian pipelines. The absence between them was long enough that he had yet to meet my youngest brother Paul, who was 14 months old.

The trip was important enough for me to have a new dress, powder-blue wool with smocking across the bodice. I could run my fingers along the silky threads that held together tiny pleats, like reading braille. Everything was new—patent leather Mary Janes, white socks, and immaculate little white gloves. Plunging my fingers into their snugness, I was the only little girl who could have such perfect gloves. I wanted to wear them the whole time, but Mama said "no, they will get dirty or lost," so they spent most of the trip in her patent leather handbag that matched my shoes. My shoes were so new and slippery I had to be careful walking.

Miniature fairy tale towns and countryside fanned out under me as I stared fascinated from the airplane window. Food laid out on trays. New coloring books and crayons just for this occasion, the hum of the airplane engines lulled and excited me. I would see my father, absent so long. He would hug me. He would be so happy to see me in my blue dress and white gloves!

It was pitch dark in LaGuardia. Moving lights outside the huge windows reflected against the night. High heels clip-clopped the marble floors. People dressed for travel in suits and hats, gloves and scarves, were going every direction. We waited on a big round couch with no armrests, stretched, then walked and walked.

Another airplane, the window again as I slept across the Atlantic. Then morning in Paris. My dress was scratchy, more hustle bustle handholding, must not get lost. Mama had to take care of papers at the long desk. "You come with me Jane, hold my hand and be good." I could and would be so very good, keeping eyes wide and only looking and listening. Strange talking echoed in garbled waves from the ceiling

"David, you watch Paul, and don't let him run. I want you to make sure he stays right here with our luggage. I have to talk to that man right over there, see? Ok?"

"Ok Mama." I was glad to be going with her.

Suddenly, Paul's screams of distress rose above the chaos. We turned to see David sitting on the baby's chest trying to muffle his noise. Then we ran, Mama let go, must not get lost. She comforted Paul, scolded David, forgot me. But I stayed close no matter what.

Paris overnight in a small hotel room, one bed, a crib and couch. We ate ham sandwiches, bathed and got ready for the final leg. In the deep tub with bird feet holding a ball, Paul turned the scalding hot water onto his face and burned his mouth and neck. This was the face his father would see for the first time—angry bubbles and wet yellow scabs.

Nothing would ruin my reunion with blue dress and gloves. Soon he would lift me up and twirl me in circles like Uncle Bobby did. He would toss me in the air and make me shriek with joy. He would hold me close against his cheek, put me on his lap, smooth my hair over my ear, and tell me what a pretty and good girl I was.

Beirut airport was startlingly bright. There were no shadows at mid-day. Clear skies and palm trees welcomed a soft breeze, and the sun had its way with everything. My eyes squinted, searching the crowd for my hero, my daddy. There he was! Handsome in his white linen jacket and pants, he wore a Panama fedora cocked to the side, same as his smile. We three ran to him.

"Daddy! Daddy! Daddy! See my gloves?"

He wrapped his arms around Mama, smoothed her jet black hair from her face, then cried as he took Paul from her, continuing to shift his attention from Mama to Paul, Mama to Paul.

"I can't believe you are here. You are finally here! David you are my little man. Did you help your mother?" Once again, he turned to Paul in his arms cooing, "Poor little guy. Poor little wounded soldier."

"Daddy, I have gloves, see my gloves?" I waved my hands frantically to capture his attention. Maybe he said "yes" and I didn't notice.

He bent down to address David. "You are such a big boy!"

Then we all piled into the shade of our car, driver in front. Daddy was in the middle with Paul on his lap, one hand secured him at his belly, the other rested on Mama's shoulder. David sat at his side. I was far away craning my face around Mama, trying one last time. "DADDY! See my gloves. Look!" I said, reaching on the edge of my seat. He gave Mama a long movie kiss.

Melting into hot silent tears, I sat back into the seat and looked out the window.

Soon Lebanon became my paradise, my garden of Eden. Sidon, our town means "to fish" but it was actually named for its founder, the first-born son of Canaan. This ancient town, 2000 years older than Christ was the promised land, the prize of kings Solomon and Nebuchadnezzar. Conquered by too many to name, she still stood her ground in 1951 on a promontory over-looking the blue Mediterranean. Here, I splashed bare-foot in the courtyard fountain with my brothers. I ran free with my nanny Angel, picking snails after the rain.

We were surrounded by the smells of flatbread baking, wild oregano and orange blossoms. Bougainville spilled over the rock walls. Sheep and goats grazed the scrub between the olive trees. Bedouins came, watered their camels, gathered sticks for their cook fires and pitched camp on the street. The holy earth was soaked with the blood of martyrs. The Adhan call to prayer three times a day was as dependable as the sun. Even at my young age, I knew the *ya habib* was meant to remind everyone that God was watching over us.

Our home, a short uphill walk from town, overlooked the turquoise sea and neatly arranged olive groves, old as Jesus. We had the top of a two-story villa with tall, curtained windows facing the dusty street. A French couple lived downstairs. The floors were marble, inlaid in the pattern of a chessboard. High ceilings and brick walls, plastered and painted white, kept the house cool. A mansion by Lebanese standards, our bathroom was as big as most of the homes. We three children shared a bedroom. David slept on the top bunk; I had the bottom. Paul slept in a high brass crib until he managed to climb out. From then on, he slept in a small bed. Our room faced the sea. Our parents' room with thick red velvet curtains pulled shut against the dust and noise, faced the street. The living room and dining room stretched out alongside the bedrooms and were divided by our immense tiled bathroom. The living room was on the street side, the dining room on the ocean side. The kitchen and stairway to the back door were beside the dining room.

Our balcony fanned out at the back of the dining room and children's room. From there you could see the curve of the earth on the far horizon and the island that sheltered Sidon from the sea. Pillars and a banister of cool marble held us safe. We gathered there for many of our meals, even though we had a cedar dining room table polished slick as a mirror. We read comics sent overseas by Aunt Lou and sat in the laps of Angel and her older sister Sumera, who thumbed through picture books and made up stories to go with them. On the sunny balcony we scooped hummus with flat bread, ate olives, dates and cucumbers, sweet as apples.

When the Mediterranean rainfall came, we rushed to the balcony to watch the sky cry. *El denya beteshty,* it's raining! This was Angel and Sumera's excited exclamation. And so, we learned more Arabic from the sisters. Paul ran in circles repeating *beteshty! beteshty!* When Daddy came home, little Paul was still chanting and doing his rain dance. Daddy accused him of cursing until we convinced him Paul was just saying rain.

It wasn't long before we kids were speaking fluently, translating for the tradesmen and beggars who came to the back door. Mama never said no to beggars, which meant long lines behind our house until Daddy put a stop to it. Paul would steal away to join the other beggar children at the brick ovens across the street. There, people brought trays of raw flatbread, baguettes and loaves to bake. *"Hubbers, hubbers,"* he pleaded, until someone would put a fresh baked piece in his chubby hand. When he was discovered, Sumera always carried him home, gently explaining he was well fed and didn't need to beg for bread.

Angel and Sumera were the daughters of Fadwa, our cook. We belonged to Mama and Daddy, but Sumera and Angel belonged to us. Paul crawled in and out of Sumera's lap, hanging from her neck. She never tired of swinging and rocking him. She put her face in his belly making him giggle and squeal.

At five, David was a pensive child accustomed to his own world of fantasy and comic books. He spent much time in solitude, marching with a stick, building an empire, swinging high and wild on the swing set. He made a makeshift Jungle Jim on the swing set by balancing a 2 x 4 in the A braces. The middle swing was shortened and served as a trapeze swing where he hung by his knees. One day he fell and cut a V-shaped gash on his head which stayed with him the rest of his life. Often the frightened sisters coaxed or bribed him down, only to find him scaling the ancient rock wall that divided our yard from the olive groves.

Fadwa prepared recipes that Mama gave her; pot roast, fried chicken, corned beef, and pinto beans cooked slow. Mama even had her roast a turkey at Christmas, using dry French baguettes for stuffing. We children much preferred the Arabic food and eating with our hands. The flavors of garlic, oregano, olive oil, chickpeas, tahini, eggplant, cucumbers, dates, and oranges were our familiars. For Christmas from the US, we got Hershey Bars and bubble gum, lemon drops, peppermint candy canes, and gold coins that were chocolate inside.

Sidon pronounced sigh-ee-dah in Arabic was always followed by a cluck at the back of the throat and a lift of the chin. This signified love for the place. No other town was ever spoken of in this way, but people were. Angel made the same gesture while bending on her haunches, her soft hands spread wide. I would run to her, knowing I was cherished and protected better than any adult, including my parents. Enveloped in her rocking embrace, I found the meaning of refuge.

When my father thought he needed to spank us, she stood firm in the face of his anger. I cowered, clinging to the back of her legs, barely brave enough to look at his face. "You have to kill me first before you touch this child." Many years later, I would learn she was only fifteen when she took that stand, willing to die for my safety. This act always shamed my father into begrudging dismissal. My brothers were equally shielded by Sumera. Daddy, pretending to be amused, made the ordeal into a joke, saving face, sparing us. Angel and Sumera took us to the balcony or outside to play, and soothed us into forgetfulness.

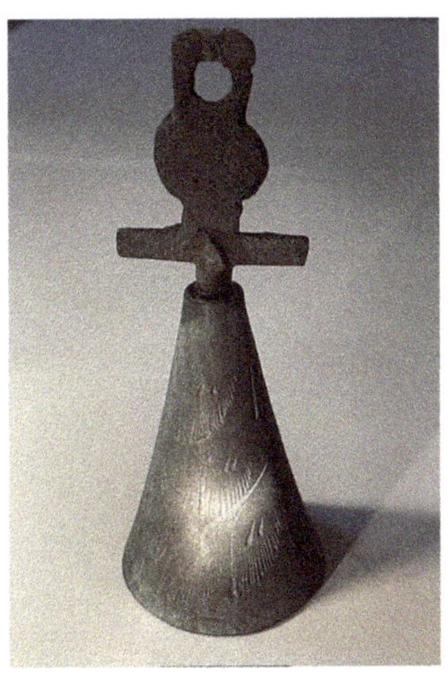

Antique Bell from Lebanon

One Sunday we went to Angel's church, orthodox Christian. We held hands. Mine fit perfectly in the cradle of her palm. The church door looked more like the entrance of a mine carved into the side of the rock.

The entrance was too small for this holy place. As we entered the sanctuary, our eyes adjusted to the light. The pungent smell of frankincense filled my nostrils. Shafts of colored light beamed into the chapel from stained glass windows. The warm golds and reds, cool blues and greens painted the people and pews, carpet and altar. Divided down the middle by a long aisle, the pews were arranged on either side, a dozen deep.

I was acutely aware of the sanctity of the place in that moment. My mind opened in innocence as I drank in the experience. I held Angel's right hand with my left, reverent. We stood at the back of the aisle ready to find our place. The priest, who stood at the altar was as startled to see me as I was to see him. He had blue eyes and white hair and he was wearing a white robe. A brocade panel with blue embroidery draped from his shoulders. I fell headfirst into his compassionate eyes, blue as the sky. We had stopped walking. I was riveted to the spot as I witnessed the priest transform. First from a luminous man, made of blue light, into a pillar of silvery-blue lightening. My body tingled, heart pounded. I knew if I took my eyes off the column of light, it would once again become a man. I held out as long as I could, awestruck. Some part of me knew this pure light.

Finally, the spell broke. He was once again the blue-eyed priest. My shoulders settled as we moved halfway up and I sat on Angel's right side. I was on the aisle. I didn't understand the words. He was not speaking

Arabic or English. But I followed his gestures and movements at the altar. He poured water, rang a bell, and slowly waved a burning ball of incense. Smoke billowed from the brass filigree ball at the end of the chain. His voice was strong and kind. His hands soared like seabirds. They came together at his chest and flew out and up to the end of his reach. He knew me. I knew him and was grateful I came.

When mass ended, Angel took my hand once again. She put her rosary into her dress pocket. She had only two dresses, an everyday dress and one for church. I was wearing my good blue dress. My white gloves didn't fit anymore. The people moved in a line, each greeted by the priest as they left. He bent to his knee when we came to say goodbye. He spoke directly to me in Arabic, "Shukan." He thanked me for coming. My cheeks reddened. I looked at my shoes and hid behind Angel.

The sun, so bright in contrast to the inside took time to get used to. We walked in silence."

"How did you like church?" she asked.

"I saw God," I answered.

"Of course you did, we were in God's house."

I was smiling to myself, satisfied that my churchgoing was shared and witnessed by my wonderful friend. It was nothing out of the ordinary, but special all at once. We skipped uphill, joyful. When we reached home, I ran ahead to report to Mama before the excitement wore off. Racing up the stairs to the kitchen,

I called out to Mama. "I saw God! Just now in church!" Mama turned her head to the side almost facing me. "That's nice honey." Suddenly I darted back to the stairway to find Angel.

One afternoon, a Bedouin caravan stopped close to our house and circled their camels in a clearing to camp for the night. We watched at a distance as they pitched tents and started their cook fires. A woman squatted, stirring with a wooden spoon. Angel saw my fascination, so she took me to the downstairs kitchen door and asked me to wait for a surprise. I waited, wondering what new adventure she had in store for me. She came racing down with a wooden spoon, water jug, and saucepan. She explained we needed to make something. "First, we need to gather fuel." We raced through the olive grove picking up dead sticks and leaves. Whenever we gathered anything, snails, arugula or wild oregano, Angel tied a square cloth over the shoulder and around her waist, hung slack at her back until it was filled by our stuffing our find in the open sides at her flanks. By the time we finished, she had a load on her back.

We took the load to the side of the street. Angel took off her burden and began to arrange the dry tinder in a tent shape. I started helping, first leaves, then small and then bigger sticks, arranging them just so. "Now go to the back door and get the jug." My job was done in a flash, so proud to be a part of this mysterious chore. The jug was a smaller version of the ones the women caried on their heads. I didn't know what was next. Angel reached into her apron pocket for a book of matches, struck and held the flame to the crushed leaves at the bottom of our stick tent. The fire danced to life, first with a ribbon of smoke until the leaves burned off. A crackling red and yellow campfire just like the nomads made.

She handed me the wooden spoon and saucepan. "Fill this with dirt to here," she said, and pointed her finger one third from the bottom. Another job for me, but it was play as I spooned the dirt into its place, then the jug. "Can you pour the water, slow into the pan?"

"Yes!"

Holding the jug like a baby in my arms, I bent my whole body to pour.

"Stop! That's enough."

I barely got started. And then Angel took the handle of the pan, gathered her apron edge into a makeshift potholder, and put the saucepan over the flames.

I was stunned. We weren't pretending. We were tending a real fire. "Now Jane, pick up the spoon and stir." In awe, I stirred the mud mix as it began to boil. Little mouths formed in the mud, opened to spit steam, and closed again as others opened, faster, thicker, louder. Angel took a stick from the unused pile and with her free hand swept the fire into a tighter circle. The little fire was burning down. The mud had thickened and become hard to stir. "Almost ready," Angel announced, as she removed the pot from the fire.

She spooned out a dob of mud onto the ground, and another until the pan was empty. "Now we have to let these cool before we can make bread." She gingerly took the first dough ball and rolled it in the dirt, coating it in dry earth, then patted it down with a spoon. "You can make the next one Jane." We made a neat row, six perfect loaves. Angel made a crisscross design with the side of the spoon.

When I think back, it occurs to me that this was the first time I had watched and been a part of the cooking. In my house, the top of the stove was in another atmosphere, inaccessible to a child. She knew all of this and knew the thrill I would experience. She seemed to live to give me joy.

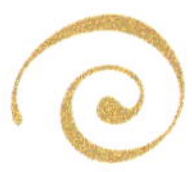

Texas
Silsbee and Fort Stockton
1950s

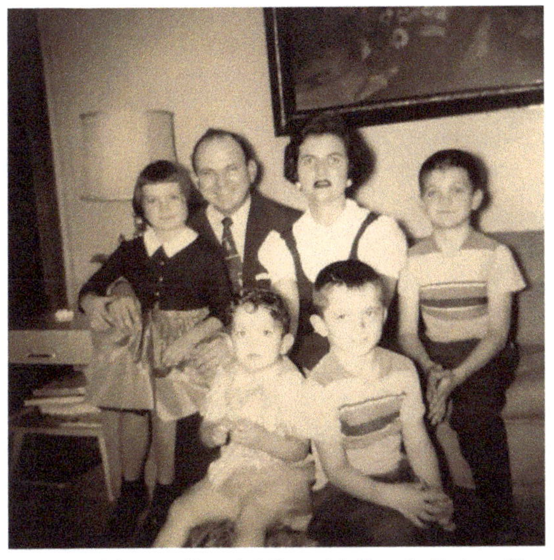

Me, Dad, Mom, David (back) Paul, John (front)
Silsbee 1955

My family's time in Lebanon abruptly came to an end the morning the charred remains of a car lay upside down like a dead bug across the street. An event we kids slept through the night before.

The sting of returning to the US was quelled by a cruise on the Queen Mary. In Gibraltar, Dad bought me a doll as big as me for a birthday party in the nursery filled with balloons. When Mom and Dad came to get we three with our treasured balloons, they took us to the deck for home movies—the wind ripping the balloons from our hands and out to sea.

Our final destination was Silsbee; a small town tucked in the piney woods of southeast Texas. We went from the top floor of the villa to a small three-bedroom tract house on a cul-de-sac. Silsbee was divided by railroad tracks; all the dark people lived on one side. I only knew one, her name was May, and she came once a week to iron. She wouldn't let me in her lap. She showed me the inside of her hands where it was so much lighter than the rest of her. She was sad.

Dad had a new job at Tinkles Furniture owned by a Navy buddy. This was the foreign land, not Lebanon. The air smelled like pine tar from a sawmill nearby, so close we could hear the high whine of the saws. We could also hear train whistles, which always gave me a wistful, lonely feeling.

Gramma and Grampa Carter lived only a few miles away on a farm in Warren, Texas in the house Daddy grew up in. Grampa is Daddy's stepfather and married Gramma when Daddy was already grown.

Before we went to Lebanon, Gramma and Grampa Carter lived in Fort Stockton, Texas. I remember Grampa's fingers were yellow brown. He would give me his lap and creep his fingers inside me. He rolled his own cigarettes and held them between his index finger and thumb when he smoked. Daddy always said he was a real southern gentleman.

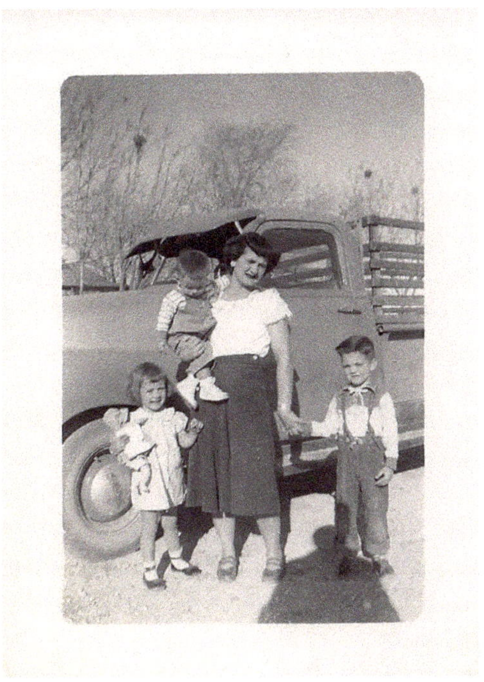

Paul with Mom, Me (l) David (r)
Fort Stockton

I remember being there on the sheep farm. There was a high windmill and a big round water trough we used to swim in. You could wander on the desert and never be lost because of the windmill.

I loved a little lamb that was just my size, soft and white. It was kept inside a corral outside the kitchen door that Gramma let me into. The lamb ran from me, but when I caught it, I would hug it. After a day or two, it didn't run, and we made friends. On the last day of our visit, I went outside to see my friend and the corral was empty. Gramma was making biscuits in the kitchen when I asked her if she knew where my friend was.

"Oh, honey that little critter needs to be with its mama."

"But where is its mama? Can we go see her?"

"No darlin' we can't," she said.

"But why gramma, why can't we?" I begged.

"That's enough now, you go outside and play Jane."

I knew I would never see my friend again as my stomach tightened with grief. I noticed a burlap bag that was hung from the mesquite tree in the back yard. It was bloody at the bottom and gave off the smell of drying blood. I never saw that before.

That night Gramma made fried lamb chops, green beans, mashed potatoes, biscuits and gravy. She made a peach pie for dessert. No amount of cajoling could get me to eat dinner.

We were once again back in Texas, but this time living in Silsbee. To visit Gramma and Grampa on their farm in Warren, we kids were piled into the back of a furniture truck with furniture blankets for the weekend rides to visit them. If Lebanon was paradise, this was hell. I missed Angel. In my innocence, I always took Grampa's lap, tricked by the strange amnesia of what would happen next. I had forgotten his tobacco-stained fingers, his bulging jeans, how his cigarette-stained fingers crawled inside of me. I forget what happened when I was left alone with him. But the bathroom was a horror-filled place, I still remember in nightmares.

When it was unbearably hot on the East Texas farm, Grampa filled a galvanized laundry tub with water from the hose so we kids could play in it. The boys and I, in our underpants, rough-housed and splashed 'til the water got shallow and Grampa would fill it again. Finally, when it was time to get out and dry off our sunburned bodies, Grampa got towels and wrapped me in a white fluffy one. His breath and his whole body smelled of cigarettes. He carried me back to the old wooden chair where he had been sitting in the shade. The boys ran into the house, screen door banging behind them. He faced me outward on his lap and started in. I put my hands on his blue jean thighs and tried to lift myself up and away. I didn't want that and started to squirm— stomach tight, fear creeping in. But I didn't get off his lap. Shame held me down like a heavy blanket. My face got hot and red. Then I let go, sank into his fumbling. Surrendered to it. It felt good. A feverish wave flooded through my six-year-old body.

When I woke from the fever dream, he put me down. I ran toward the house, felt the prickly grass under my feet, smelled pine sap and saw the dark piney woods all around me. I wanted to run into the shade and safety there and would have if I hadn't been so afraid of getting lost.

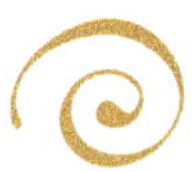

Elvis at the Bus Stop
Thousand Oaks

1960

That day was no different, perfectly ordinary—until I saw Elvis at the bus stop. The school bus took forty minutes from Thousand Oaks High School to Lake Sherwood fire station. I took off my makeup and let down the French roll ratted into my hair. It wouldn't take forty minutes, but close. Baby oil takes off mascara. I would roll down the waistband of my skirt when I got off the bus. This was my ritual, putting on the makeup and doing my hair on the way to school, undoing everything on the way home.

Connie West wore mascara from the start. She wore so much that her eyelashes looked like spiders' legs. Her mom was an actress and didn't disapprove of makeup. We were 15, obsessed with all things teenage, especially Elvis and the Beatles.

When the bus hissed its way to my stop, I saw a circle of black-clad motorcycle guys smoking cigarettes and laughing. They were circled around one particular guy with Elvis Presley hair. Wait, it was Elvis! Those eyes! Those lips!

The excitement had me shaking. Could make me mute. I must talk to him. My legs quivering, I made it off the bus and stood frozen, mind racing. Go-go-go over there. I was stuck to the ground. My voice and feet failed me. I squeezed my books to my heart and unstuck the first step. My robotic march to the circle had started. Five short yards.

"Mr. Presley, could I please have your autograph?" Don't faint, don't fall, don't stutter. Don't cry, and don't scream.

"Why sure darlin. You have a paper and pen?"

The other guys kind of snickered, which threatened to freeze me up again.

"You boys settle down. What's your name sweetheart?"

"Um, uh . . . Jane." I fumbled with my binder, tried to get it open without dropping my books.

"Let me take the books," he offered, in a soft southern drawl.

Don't swoon, don't faint, don't cry. Give him your books and get a piece of paper. My fingers didn't work. My face was hot. Finally, I ripped a paper from the three-hole binder.

He took the paper and pen, put the paper on top of my books and wrote, then handed me the paper and books with a dazzling smile.

"Thank you," I said, cheeks hot, heart pounding, I turned towards my walk home. The rest of the kids were standing there staring. My brothers, Gerald Houser, and Will Borgeson stood transfixed, even hypnotized. I stopped and looked down at my paper cradled on my books.

To Jane, love Elvis Presley. Don't cry in front of the boys. Don't turn around. Keep walking. Don't run. I could feel eyes on me. Sorry I didn't have makeup, but my skirt was still short. Was I pretty?

I joined the boys who wanted to see the autograph. I was afraid of teasing or tearing up, so I ran. Most of the mile home, I ran.

"Mom! Mom! Elvis Presley is at the bus stop!"

"Oh yes, one of my Fuller Brush customers told me they're filming a motorcycle movie in Hidden Valley." She leaned in conspiratorially and whispered, "Let's go see if we can get another glimpse of him. Just let me change."

I had forgotten to let my skirt down and she hadn't even noticed. I went to my room and brushed my hair, put a little water on the brush to get the kinks out, and put on some Tangee lipstick, which was allowed. What else could I get away with? Mascara?

Mom came out wearing her good white pedal pushers and a sleeveless red and white checked shirt tied at the midriff. She had put on makeup and done her hair.

"Ok, you ready?" she said. "Let's go."

"Mom, you look so nice."

"I just cleaned up a bit."

I was wearing a green plaid skirt, as short as possible (that Mom had yet to notice), and a white shirt. She didn't say a thing about my appearance.

"Where are the keys to the station wagon?"

We had a woody before it was the rage. Whenever Mom came to pick us up, we made her park outside the school driveway. I always ducked down 'til we were out of range.

"You think the boys want to go?" she asked.

"No Mom, just me and you. They're still walking from the bus stop."

"We can ask them when we see them on the road," she said.

"Ugh!"

Mom looked nice. I wasn't embarrassed, at least not then. I started to feel the nervous shake in my stomach. My hands were getting clammy wondering if I could look into those sparkly blue eyes again. We drove around the lake, no sign of the boys. Maybe they took the upper road.

"Shall we stop by Cathy's house and see if she wants to go?"

"No Mom, she's at band practice and Caren is at cheerleading practice. There were no girls at the bus stop today."

"Ok, just me and you, then."

She made a left turn at the fire station onto Hidden Valley Road. Joel McCrea had a horse ranch out here as did Eve Arden, Connie's mom. I've had sleepovers there.

They had a live-in maid who served us after-school snacks. She had every record we loved. We wound through the valley to the ranch.

"The headquarters is at the barn. Let's go find him."

"Mom, wait, I feel funny."

"Take a deep breath and get yourself together. He puts his pants on one leg at a time just like everybody else."

I remembered her telling me about meeting Frank Sinatra when she was a teenager. She knew what she was talking about.

The barn doors were wide open and there was a bunch of people milling around, lots of parked cars (Cadillacs), motorcycles, trucks, and buses. In the center, around the big cameras, were deck chairs with names on the back. I reached for Mom's hand. There was his chair! Elvis Presley! He was sitting in it, and a few people were standing around earnestly talking. Mom barreled right through, still holding my hand.

"Mr. Presley, we don't want to bother you, but we wanted to say hello. I'm Vaye Jean Watkins and this is Jane."

"Well now, Jane, I see you brought your sister." Big smile, stretching those full lips across his perfect teeth, sparkly blue eyes looking straight into mine. I was glad to still be holding Mom's hand. She was blushing, looking down for a beat, then up with renewed resolve.

"Can we trouble you for your autograph?"

"My pleasure, ladies."

Mom reached into her purse and pulled out a notepad. She was prepared.

"How do you spell your name?"

"Vaye Jean is my whole name."

She spelled out Vaye. He got the rest and wrote, *To Vaye Jean, love Elvis.*

"One more please," Mom almost whispered.

"Oh, I already have one."

"I'll give you a spare." He winked and wrote, *All the best, Elvis Presley.*

I was standing close enough to examine his eyes, transfixed. He had eyeliner and mascara. I didn't realize he was handing me the paper.

"Thank you," I choked, stuck to the ground.

"We need you on set, Mr. Presley," someone called.

"Uh huh, coming."

Mom unstuck me by pulling on my hand.

"Thank you so much for taking the time, Mr. Presley."

"You girls call me Elvis."

I hated to go, to get back in the car and normal life. Our pace quickened as we got closer to the car.

"He is even more handsome in real life," Mom said.

"I know, and so nice."

We watched a lady comb his hair and powder his face while he sat.

"I love him," I announced.

"Well, he's just so lovable," said Mom.

The next day after school, I hopped on my bike and rode out to the Hidden Valley Ranch just to catch a glimpse. The whole production was gone. Was it just a dream? And yet Paramount Studios filmed the movie *Roustabout* in 1964, a motorcycle movie starring Elvis Presley.

Sadly, the autographs never made it into scrapbooks and were eventually lost in the chaos of moving. Except for the spare, that I gave to my best friend Marilyn Musgraves, who has kept it folded in a square in her wallet to this day. *All the best, Elvis Presley.*

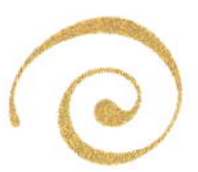

Dad
Lake Sherwood
1964–68

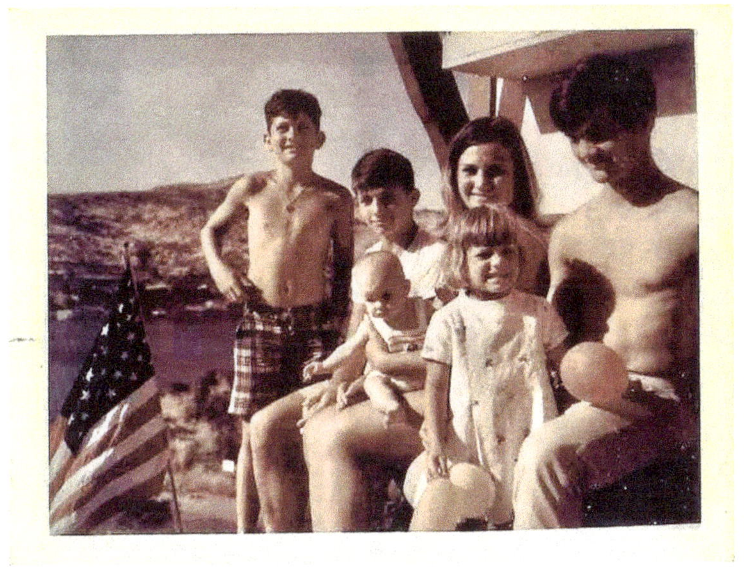

Watkins Kids at Lake Sherwood

High school years 1964-68 were marked by the ever-widening rift between my father and me. He complained about that "troublemaker" Martin Luther King almost nightly at the dinner table, while I thought King was noble and brave. I was naive and ignorant and didn't know a damn thing about this country because I hadn't fought in the war, wasn't a grown up, and didn't have a responsible or respectful bone in my body. I was shamed to my room to cry hot angry tears of confusion and rage. I also had the absurd notion that the war in Vietnam seemed ill advised. As it was televised nightly in our living room, children immolated, villages burned to the ground, napalm everywhere. I was once again part of the problem, unpatriotic lefty.

The rift widened to an impassable chasm, marked by shaming, shouting, and scoffs. I went on to be the bleeding-heart liberal I am today, and Dad was a bible-thumping Rush Limbaugh-loving conservative, who rewrote history at every turn. Then would tell you he always believed in Dr. King. I was there for God's sake! How does one live in a world where history can be retold to convenience? How does one make peace with being ashamed of one's own father? I want to love him. I don't.

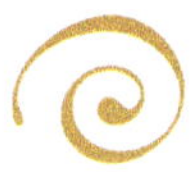

Summer of '66
Big Sur to Pennsylvania
1966

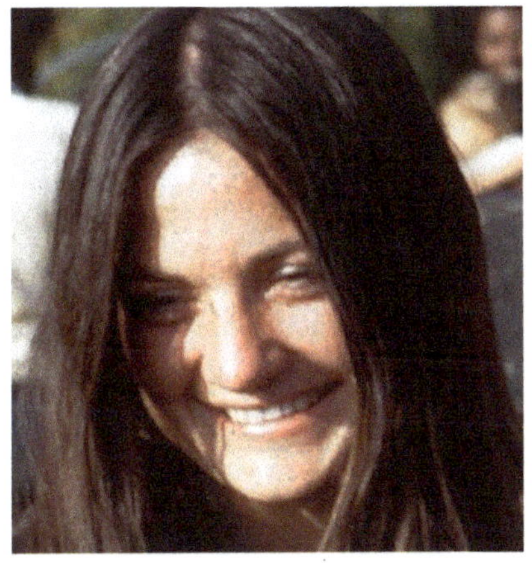

Me

Freshman year started well, English honors and class president. Then I had a beer, smoked a joint, took LSD, and it all went downhill. I barely graduated. Strawberry fields beckoned. The hippie commune, tucked in Decker Canyon tempted me to ditch high school since my junior year. Either paradise found or Dante's *Inferno*, depending on the trip I was on.

At 18, in the summer before the summer of love, I couldn't escape Thousand Oaks fast enough. Strawberry fields lured me, twenty minutes from my house. An old ranch bought by a Jesus-wanna-be, Gridley Wright, stockbroker turned cult leader. He, except for his arrogance, nailed the role of Dr. Kildare playing the part of Christ. Commanding height, chiseled features, flowing mane, robe and sandals. Sermons were delivered in an open stable on a bale of hay—the gospel of turn on, tune in, and drop out.

Everyone had a handle—Turtle, Rainbow, Meadow, Gypsy. True to my disregard for myself and appalling taste in men, I chose my mate, Hostile John, an ex-con visiting from some flop house in Venice, and probably the most dangerous resident of Strawberry Fields. Sitting in a circle around the campfire, passing a joint, and out of the blue, WHACK! A stinging slap across my face. Being no stranger to the humiliation of a face slap, I deep-down figured I deserved it and stuck it out.

Once, on a hellish paranoid trip, I hopped into my little purple VW bug with the obligatory floral paint job. My plan to escape was hampered by taking my horrified psyche with me. The twisting road through the canyon writhed with snakes bearing their fangs from all sides. Escape thwarted, I returned the few yards I had traveled, back to the bedlam of sixty people peaking on lysergic acid diethylamide.

An older woman calmly approached. She asked how could she help, what did I need? Not yet comatose with fear, I heard myself say the word "security." She paused, took my shoulders in her hands, looked me in the eyes.

"The only security you will ever find in this world is knowing there is none."

"Far out."

It soothed me. I came back to my body and the sound of Jim Morrison singing "C'mon Baby Light My Fire". Quite possibly an omen since the place burned to the ground on Easter Sunday, 1966. After the fire, I started visiting the "older" woman Zelita. The willowy 21-year-old ballet dancer and painter had a house on Heart Street in Venice. The soul of loving kindness, her view of me was far above that of my own.

A friend of Zelita's, Bob, ancient man of 30, came to visit on Heart Street. He was a schoolteacher, tall, scruffy, spoke like a beatnik. Everything groovy and cool, he invited us on a road trip. His destination, Millbrook, New York to teach school in Timothy Leary's experimental society. Heady stuff for this fledgling hippie girl. I would go anywhere with Zelita!

Up Highway 1, our first stop Avila Beach, to collect 500 hits of acid, cooked up by a Mad Max, Cal Poly science student. After sampling his latest batch, we left the next day stopping in San Louis Obispo to harvest avocados and oranges from the Cal Poly orchards.

In Big Sur, hippie caravans camped on Highway 1 above Esalen. We joined the Mecca.

My first experience in Esalen's hot springs took me back to a former life, a Nordic life where people were

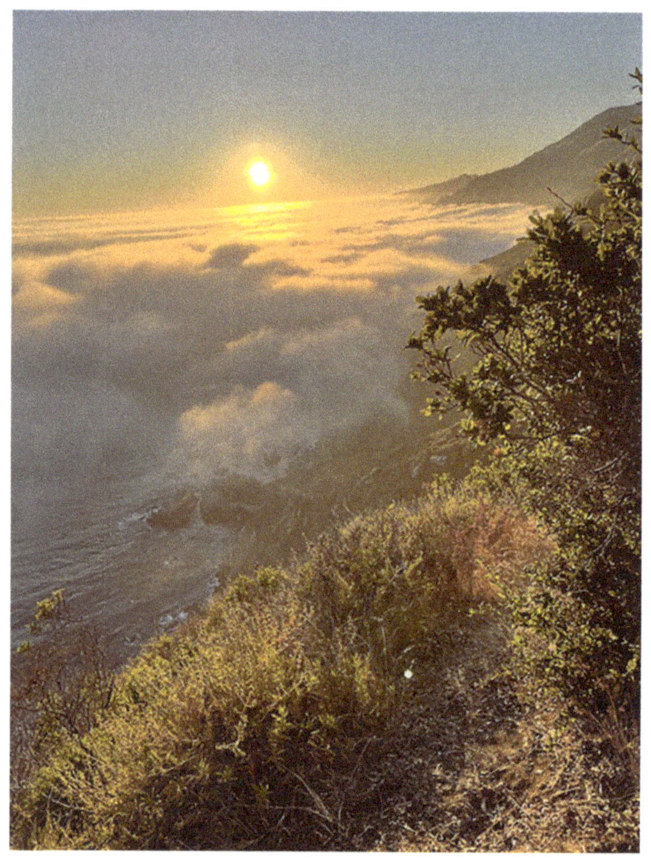

Big Sur

buxom, healthy, and unashamed of their bodies. A golden light surrounded the vision of the warm sulfur springs, serene. In Big Sur, we picked up 300 peyote buttons, a kilo each of hash and weed. With our summer supply of psychedelics, we spent the night on Partington Ridge with a family Bob knew in a beautiful cabin overlooking the vast pacific. After dinner, I boxed and gift wrapped our stash with the words *Happy High* on the wrapping. The next morning, with Bob in our Volkswagen van, we three wound down the ridge back to Highway 1 and headed north.

Bay Area Food Mill, the hugest health food store known to man, would supply our culinary needs. We bought pounds of brown rice, chamomile tea, millet, lentils, alfalfa, and sunflower seeds, each wrapped in brown paper. We got dried plums, figs, apricots, raisins, almonds, walnuts, and peanuts.

In San Francisco, we crashed with a friend of Bob's in a two-story house in Haight Ashbury. Jack, a quiet gentle man, taught me the *I Ching*, made me feel smart the way he explained the coins, the hexagrams.

"The Sage is the god within. He is your inner guide. You can always trust him to keep you on course. You dig?"

"Heavy, man," I dug.

From there, we headed cross-country on US 50, cutting through the heartland in Bedouin garb, long hair and love beads. We camped, drove, ate avocados and oranges. Passing through Utah, I started to weep.

"What's bringing you down?" Bob asked.

"Aw sweetie wha's wrong?" Zelita said.

I just shook my head, bewildered.

"She misses her mama," Bob suggested, which brought on another wave. My mother, father, brothers and sisters and former life drifted further and further behind.

We got to Pennsylvania when the van broke down. Bob's old girlfriend from Big Sur, Sylvia, lived with a mechanic in town. He towed the van to his house with his pickup. Zelita and I took our bags, the stolen credit card we got in Big Sur from a guy named Robot, and checked in to Howard Johnsons.

Luxury was lolling in the bathtub pretending we were at Esalen. Bob took a Greyhound to Millbrook for his teaching gig. We ate motel food, smoked a joint and slept on clean sheets. The next morning, we dropped acid. Just as we were coming on, we got a call from Sylvia's boyfriend telling us our bus was ready to drive upstate, and we could pick it up. Zelita wrote down the address and we called a cab. At twilight we arrived at the mechanics. Detectives, local sheriffs, and federal agents were everywhere. Was I hallucinating? A uniformed sheriff opened the cab door, told us to get our bags from the trunk and come with them. Cowering in the back of a black and white, we held hands all the way to Greensburg federal prison. The moon watched us, and we watched her. When we got out, I got the feeling I wasn't hallucinating, which sent a bolt of white-hot fear through my body.

In a harshly lit room, Zelita and I sat side by side at an aluminum table. Questions about the drugs and who was driving came at us.

"You are me, I am you, we are all together," I said.

The detective blinked, smirked. Valiant, Zelita stood, went to her suitcase and pulled out her personal stash.

"If I give you this, will you arrest me and let her go?"

We were summarily arrested and separated. Quivering with fear I was told to strip naked.

I called out a plaintive, "ZELITA!?"

"JANE!" she echoed.

Through a shower of lye soap, fingerprinting, mug shots, and a tiny holding cell we continued the call and response deep into the night.

Out the window of my holding cell, in a small patch of dirt, a yellow dandelion peeked up. That's me. I was coming down hard to this grim reality. I was definitely there, in a federal prison in the Quaker state. Greensburg had automated doors, a central command station, and cameras everywhere. A matron escorted me to my cell. I wore the women's uniform; a wrap dress printed with tree houses and signs saying *Our Happy Home*. I had to get out of that dress and that place. Bigger than the holding cell, my cell had a camera that peered down from the corner, a cot, and a toilet. I called out for Zelita again. She answered.

The next day I slept as long as possible, hoping I'd wake in my lavender bedroom with the window by my bed. The matron came with the local newspaper. We made the frontpage headline. BIGGEST DRUG BUST IN THE HISTORY OF PENNSYLVANIA. A dozen smug-looking police stood behind a table piled with not only our happy-high contents, but all our purchases from the food mill. My heart sank to the pit of my guts.

Our public defender, just out of college, met with us in a brown suit one size too tight. He told me not to pull a Timothy Leary, which I didn't understand. He then further explained that I should not speak well of drugs, that I would be easier to defend if I was sorry. I was sorry alright.

Prison life unfolded at a tedious pace. Mornings we lined up in front of our cells and marched to the day room, a large cage in the heart of the women's side. Breakfast was served on aluminum trays, at aluminum tables with aluminum benches. I embarked on a hunger strike for no reason except suicidal depression. It lasted a whopping one week 'til I was threatened with solitary confinement. After cleaning that cell, no bars, just a steel box, I decided to have a bite of something. Breakfast, then we hung out until lunch, then after lunch, more boring hours until dinner, more time to kill until we were marched back to our cells to wait for lights out. The only variations to this theme were work details, church on Sunday, and a weekly one-hour visit to the day yard. Concrete with three 12-foot walls connected to the west wall of the prison, stood as our federally mandated recreational area. Not a blade of grass in sight. Zelita and I would lie on our backs, cup our hands around the sides of our eyes blocking the walls, and stare at the sky for the allotted hour. Imagining we were on a tropical island, with the ocean just a few paces away would have to feed our souls for the week.

Our fellow inmates aligned against us from the start. We, the outsiders, kept to ourselves, grateful to have each other. One inmate killed her husband by separating him from his manhood in his sleep with a machete. Another drowned her children in a bathtub, five of them. I was never sure if she accomplished this task all at once or knocked them off one at a time. The unsavory crowd of about a dozen women smoked and chatted all day as if in a beauty parlor. Zelita and I took a work detail mending the men's uniforms. We got to do this because we both knew how to use a sewing machine. I much preferred this to mopping the men's side while they leered, making lascivious cat calls. The work shirts and jeans were much preferred over the dresses, and we were allowed the change.

Zelita did a portrait in pencil of me looking sad and old in my uniform. I did a drawing of two roses enclosed in a thorny cage. When everyone went to the chapel on Sundays, Zelita and I exercised our freedom of religion by staying in the day room. She practiced ballet while I climbed the bars and hung by my knees from the cross-bars. We told each other stories of our lives, fantasized about where we would go if we were free. I would go to Big Sur.

One night, I woke myself up with the sound of my own sobs, my pillow slick with snot and tears. I heard myself calling for my mother, hardly recognizing my own voice. An elderly matron appeared in front of my cell. She must have heard my keening from command central. The same matron who had first escorted me to my cell. She resembled my gramma Charlotte, white hair and portly. In a kind voice, she asked me to come to her as she reached her arms through the bars. I did. I put my wet cheek against her shoulder, still sobbing. "I know you are a good girl, and I know you're scared. You are a long way from home, and you miss your mama. You remind me of my granddaughter, same age." She patted my back as she spoke. "You just got caught up with the wrong people at the wrong time, but I know you'll be all right. I don't know how I know it, but I do." The sleeve of her uniform soaked in my tears from shoulder to elbow. As my crying wound down to jagged hiccup breaths and sighs, she continued. "You just get back in your cot and trust me when I tell you it's gonna all work out. God has a plan for you, and it's not for you to be wasting away in here, I'm sure of it. Go to sleep now sweetie. God is holding you in his love."

She opened the cradle of her arms and released me. I climbed back into my cot and sunk into a deep and peaceful sleep.

My Mom found out I was imprisoned by UPI report, i.e. somebody read it in the paper. THOUSAND OAKS GIRL HELD ON DRUG CHARGES IN PENNSYLVANIA! Mom called Carol, an older cousin who lived in Pittsburg. I wasn't expecting a visit when the women's guard called my name. "Watkins you have a visitor." Gates opened automatically as I walked bewildered to the front. Who could be visiting? My parents weren't coming, they couldn't afford It. Just like on TV with the glass partition and phone, there was Carol. I hadn't seen her since I was 12 at cousin Sharon's wedding. I recognized her as the Meade clan holds such a resemblance to each other. We all have strong jaws, square faces, Irish eyes, and the same wide smile. I cried when I sat down across from her. She cried too. We put our hands on the glass matching our handprints and looked into each other's eyes. She spoke first.

"Oh, my dear Janie. You must be so scared being here. I am bringing your mom's love with me. She was terribly worried when she called me." She dabbed her eyes with a wadded tissue. "I promised her I would come see you, bring you a few things to cheer you up. I guess they will inspect everything at the office before they give them to you. Everyone sends buckets of love and prayers, sweetie."

"Thank you for coming," I choked out the words.

"What does your lawyer say? Does he think you have a good case?"

"I really don't know, I have no idea." I tried to think of something hopeful to say, nothing came to mind. "Thank you so much for coming. I wish I could go home with you." This brought on another wave of tears. I looked down to see them drip on my jeans and wiped my nose on the sleeve of my work shirt.

"Times up," announced the guard.

She startled me. I cringed and stood awkwardly.

"Thank you, thanks so much."

Before I returned to my cell, I was given a package containing two books, *The Glass Bead Game* by Hermann Hesse and *The Hobbit*, spearmint gum, and a five-dollar bill. I started *The Glass Bead Game* and kept reading the same paragraph over and over. I couldn't understand it. The book made me feel stupid. I gave up on it and picked up *The Hobbit*. Like Alice down the rabbit hole, I fell completely into Middle Earth, savoring every sentence. *The Hobbit* filled my imagination and my dreams. I dreamt the ring was in my possession and I put it on and escaped, slipping through the doors with the night watch, to command central and out the door with the last of the day shift. I ran and danced over the rolling green hills outside the prison walls. I leapt with forceful bounds and bounced higher with the momentum of my impact. I leapt to the treetops and landed there to rest and study the face of the moon. I played on my own like I did at the age of eight.

Then the first light of dawn touched the horizon. I wondered which direction to run until I remembered Zelita. I couldn't leave her there alone. I had to return. I slipped back into the prison as deftly as I had escaped. I squeezed my way into my cell, took off the ring, and settled down for a little sleep before morning bell. I woke up refreshed with the secure knowledge that my soul was free and that I could dance in the moonlight again. I had flying dreams like Peter Pan flying over London. I flew high and fast from coast to coast over the sparkly towns, lakes, and mountains. I had dreams of riding a bike across the flat desert, fast and free. My bike would eventually lift up into the air and I could go anywhere.

Days turned into weeks, weeks into months. Zelita's father visited her. We had a court date set for the end of August. We both had to wear the dresses again, those ugly prison dresses with the ridiculous print. We were told by the public defender not to say anything. He would talk for us. Fine with me, I was too scared to utter a word anyway. My lawyer in the tight brown suit submitted a writ of *habeas corpus*. I had no idea what it meant. Zelita did though.

"They have to have a reason for holding us. *Habeas* is hold and *corpus* is body, a reason to hold our bodies here," she whispered.

We held hands. "Oh. But they do have a good reason, don't they?"

Brown suit glared at us. We held our whispers until the judge banged down the gavel.

"That's it then girls, you are free to go."

"What, really?" I sputtered.

Zelita threw her arms around me, so much taller that my head tucked under her chin. We were driven back to prison in the van, given our suitcases and clothes we were arrested in. Zelita's dad wired us money for the Greyhound bus, and we were off to Big Sur.

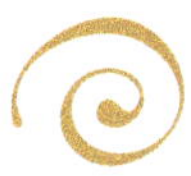

Hippies at Esalen
Big Sur
1966

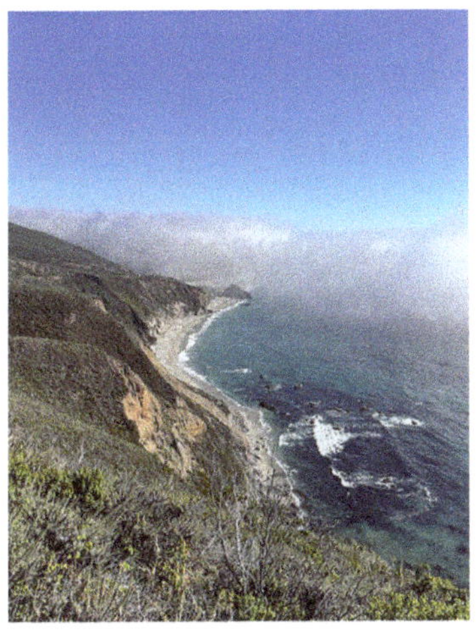

Big Sur Coastline

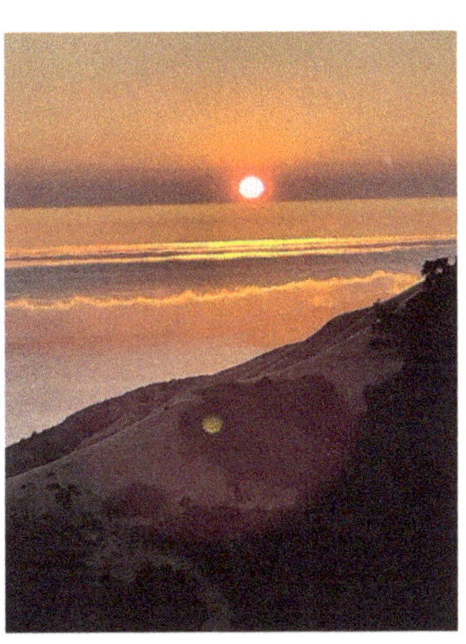

Big Sur Sunset

Hippies came to Big Sur in waves. Beatniks came first but this was our time. The 60s. They came as whoever they wanted to be depending on the costume— magicians, cowboys, pirates, Heidi the goat girl, gypsies, queens, medieval bar maids, yogis, jesters and thieves.

They tucked themselves into the beaches and canyons, converged at local spots, Redwood Lodge, Nepenthe and especially Esalen, previously Slates Hot Springs, a rustic motel and natural sulfur hot springs located six miles south of Partington Ridge, home to Henry Miller.

Esalen was the brainchild of two Stanford grads interested in what would come to be known as The Human Potential Movement. These two acquired the property and transformed it into Esalen, named for the local native tribe. Most defiant locals continued to call the place simply, Hot Springs. Notables such as Virginia Satir, Abe Maslow, Fritz Pearls, and Ida Rolf transmitted their wisdom to paying seminarians. That place drew me like the siren's song.

First thing after prison and the trip back cross-country to California, I hopped into my purple VW bug and made off for Big Sur. Zelita came with but didn't feel the magnetic pull and wound up catching a ride back to Venice.

That was where I laid my claim, there on the cliff edge above the booming sea, redwoods, eucalyptus, and creosote. In the lodge at sunset, girls in long skirts lit the candles for dinner as the sun sank into the golden Pacific. Conga drums and guitars played out by the fire pit. Love floated like otters beneath the hot baths in the sea foam. I would be one of the long-skirted beauties serving and smiling. How? First a place to crash, which meant finding someone with a bed to sleep with. First few nights were with Elliott Dunderdale, the ruddy Esalen mechanic who had a lean-to covered with tarps between two eucalyptus trees. Baths and meals were covered, so I spent my days stringing beads on the lawn in front of the lodge. When the kitchen manager, Peter Melchior, walked to work in the morning, I was there to ask for a job. "Nothing available," didn't stop me from pestering him until I landed one. Not the coveted waitress job, but cabin maid with Joellen Lapidas. I had worked as a motel maid one summer in Laguna Beach, so I knew the drill.

Finally, I got on the kitchen crew with Goph Albits, Jim and Virginia Hiriskos, and Dick Horan. Goph, a jewelry designer, had a magical hobbit house north of Hot Springs Creek. Put together with railroad ties, found objects, old windows, doors, and stained glass, a gem tucked between eucalyptus, sycamore, and live oaks. Fuchsia plants, wind chimes, prisms and crystals, hung from the lower branches.

We had three-day candle-making parties gathering around a big vat of wax scraped from the floor of a Morro Bay candle manufacturer. When all the wax was either used for elegant tapers, sand or molded candles, they were gathered into boxes and sold to the Phoenix shop at Nepenthe. Money for another party. Building code enforcement eventually tore down Goph's house. It should have been preserved.

Jim Hiriskos, a soft-spoken Greek, was the cook on the dinner shift. Laid back, his kitchen was the no-stress zone. He seemed shy until after the kitchen was cleaned up and we put on Credence Clear Water Revival or Aretha. It was then he danced like a madman, dripping with sweat long after everyone else was done.

Another hub was the art barn, situated on Esalen property's northernmost flank. A barn with a loft overlooking the sparkling Pacific. We who gathered there to produce art were the "guild of hands." Carl Lee, potter, jeweler, sage lived in the loft. He was probably in his mid-twenties with a huge walrus mustache and a mane of sandy blond hair. His voice was deep and craggy, he was ancient. John Horler, also a potter, was better known as a master batik artist. I apprenticed with John, fascinated by the medium. John looked like a wiry Liverpool docks man. Dick Horan was also a jeweler, sculptor with a sly sense of humor and a wicked smile. Alex Cane, lanky wild redhead was a leather worker and potter, who, every six months or so would gleefully hurl and crash all her seconds (imperfect pieces) into a cement raku kiln, while I begged her not to.

When we weren't working our shifts in the lodge or at the baths, we were in the art barn. Standing around the centrifugal caster waiting for the bumble bee who had flown into the batik wax to be cast in gold. We smoked bales of weed, drank wine, and laughed our faces off. We created huge batiks on Esalen sheets, later used as stage sets and backdrops for the Big Sur Folk Festivals.

After nine months or so, I was moved to the front desk with Katty Bleibtreu. Katty was wife to John Bleibtreu, dropped-out stockbroker and author of *Parable of the Beast*. Katty was a southern debutante and barefoot mother to their three boys, Josh, Adam, and Jason.

The front desk faced north, looking over the circular driveway, lawn, garden, a row of trailers housing staff, and cabins along the east edge of the property. Behind the front desk was a wall safe, its only contents a large mayonnaise jar filled with drugs. LSD for anyone who wanted to take an acid trip, Ritalin, uppers, downers and more. Owsley LSD was traded by the Grateful Dead to Esalen accountant John Ferington for keeping their books. John had a clean-shaven haircut whose only hint of weirdness was his Edwardian top hat.

By the time I made it to the front desk, I had a place of my own. The maid's quarters, a two-story addition off the kitchen of the Big House, the original homestead of the Murphy family. John Steinbeck forged his story *East of Eden* with the Murphy's in mind. Steinbeck was a friend of the family and kept correspondence with Dennis, one of their two boys, also a writer, until his death.

The Big House stood on a circular lawn just north of Esalen property. It faced a modest house on the other side of the lawn. The living room looked out over Hot Springs Creek and the ocean. Still, the maid's quarters, closest to the cliff edge had the best view.

One of my best friends was Marcia Price, wife of a race car driver. Her residence at Esalen was the result of a nervous breakdown. Tall, blond, buxom and beautiful, the only woman on the maintenance crew, she went bare-breasted digging ditches with the rest of the guys. She was crazy in love with Joel Peters, a bearded long-haired cook. Joel was quiet and shy, eventually found Marcia too much for him. He moved on but she didn't. She romanced the thought of suicide, but I never took it seriously until the day she crawled into Joel's VW bus and shot herself through the heart with Joel's hunting rifle.

Another friend, Diana Price, was in love and always fighting with her boyfriend Roger. I once tried to break them up and got a black eye for my trouble. They were together long enough to have a baby girl. One day, Diana came to the door of the art barn. I was mixing dye and melting wax for new batiks. She stood mutely in the doorway and stared at me.

"What is it, Diana? What's wrong?"

No answer, just the eerie stare. Then she bolted, I ran after her, but she disappeared into thin air. Later that day I learned she hung herself in one of the cabins. Was she really there at the art barn?

When Esalen got scary crazy, I'd pack up my little VW bug and sit in the driver's seat plotting my escape. Where to go? Maybe a hot sulfur bath would clear my head.

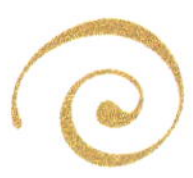

Arica
Chile
1970

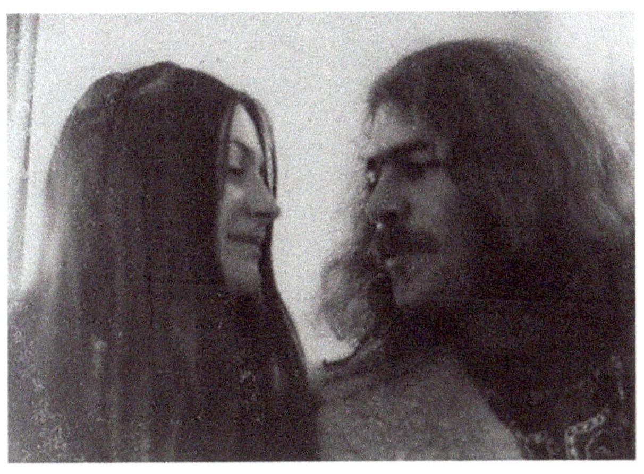

Me and Lyle

I was now set in Big Sur. My boyfriend, Lyle and I had moved from Esalen to Partington Ridge, 6 miles up the coast. We lived in the first house on the ridge. I had made it to a good life with a rich, handsome prince. Cinderella in my batik studio connected to the house. My best friends lived in the next house above us. We had a sprawling view of the Pacific Ocean. Sometimes the fog rolled in right below us and the sun lit it up like a diamond cape, or the clouds covered our house and I would have to walk up the ridge to find sunshine. Some days I walked all the way to the top of Partington Ridge to De Angulo Ranch. There lived a couple of artists and their families, the Branamans and the Halls. I'd join up with some of the six kids, pick flowers, play hide and seek, do art, or have tea with their mothers, Irene and Susan.

Word was going around in Big Sur, especially at Esalen, of a teacher, Oscar Ichazo—a Mystic. My best friend Katty Bleibtreu and her ex-husband John went to Arica, Chile to check him out. John and Katty were oil and water. They couldn't be in the same room together. Their distain palpable. Yet they went and when they came back, they were smiling and sighing. They had light bouncing out of their eyes. I absorbed Katty's joy by looking into her eyes.

So, a plan was made for Americans to form a group to study with Oscar for nine months. I was not having it. I had found my perfect life and the sound of gurus put me off. But he was going, my prince in shining armor. What a dilemma.

A gathering was arranged of 40 Americans from Big Sur to San Francisco and further. We would meet in our living room because we had the biggest meeting area of anyone in Big Sur. We formed a huge circle with a candle in the middle, Revel's "Bolero" on the turntable.

Sitting cross-legged, we put our hands together in a Prayer Mudra and said a long, deep *Ommmm*.

The exercise was to feel the flute in our spine, to feel the melody in our hearts, and to feel the drums in our lower bellies. When the music ended, we did the same *Mudra* and *Om*. I felt completely calm and grounded like a Buddha, also energized and tingly, clear and clean. I had feelings similar to tripping on LSD. It was truly remarkable and stunning. You would've thought that this cinched the deal for me. But no, my resistance was great. I would go, but I would take care of the kids.

Our trip to Arica was with John and Katty, their three boys, Samantha Cahill and Juan Salinas. Oh, and lest we forget, my big shaggy sheepdog Bianca. This was frowned on because of my attachment to a dog. I had to drag her all this way and apparently dogs have a pretty low level of consciousness. The Bleibtreu boys were taken on to our home to be.

The adults went to Oscar's house and sat in his living room carpeted with tatami mats. He sat cross-legged and welcomed us. We sat in a circle around him. He had a neat mustache, black hair, dark eyes and looked Mayan or Chinese or a mixture of both.

As he started talking in a deep voice, his hands moved gracefully through the air. The general theme was that we were asleep, our minds were full of thoughts, projections, and fears that distorted reality. The object of the training was for us to wake up. While he continued talking, I watched his profile. Suddenly, I

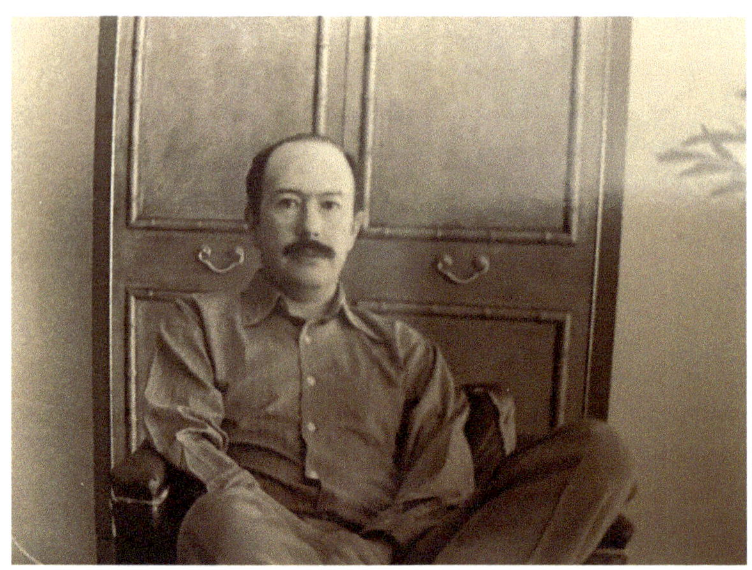

Oscar Ichazo

started to hallucinate as he became red and grew horns and a tail that snaked towards me with an inverted heart on the end. My hair stood up with fear. Then just as quickly, he transformed into white light, a robe, a long beard, and long white hair. He was blue-white light as he discussed duality and that it was an illusion. He turned and looked me straight in the eyes and said, "Get it?" I did, realizing that those two images were from my mind, a projection, the good and the bad, the dark and the light. When he finished, we sat in silence, rich and full.

"Ok, Teco and Marcos will take you home."

Samantha, Katty and I got into Teco's pick-up truck with everyone's luggage in back. We held hands—our minds were one clear space. Suddenly a thought came in. I felt it. I didn't think it, but I felt it and immediately a kid on a bike came skidding to a halt and almost hit the truck. I remembered his saying that we lived in a level of accidents because we were asleep. We returned to one clear mind again.

We were taken to a motel in the Azapa Valley and assigned rooms. John and Katty and the boys had the big house. Lyle and I had a room close to the big house. Some of our cohorts slept in tents on the property. Rowland Hall, his wife and kids stayed in a big tent. We all used the community kitchen.

Much of what we learned in Chile was based on the teachings of George Gurdjieff, a Greek American Mystic and philosopher.

The next day we were taught psycho-calisthenics, a vigorous set of exercises, including yoga poses. The teaching was in an abandoned Coca-Cola factory, then breakfast followed by meditation, mantra, and stories about the adventures of Milarepa, a Tibetan ne're-do-well who became a monk. We went to the ocean and sang to the sea, mantra in Sanskrit. In the evening after dinner, we met in a local school room. Oscar taught more theory, breathing exercises, and mantra.

Sundays were in the Atacama Desert. *Pampas* was walking, saluting the sun, carrying boulders from one point to another, and opening our arms to the sky after climbing to the top of a hill while saying to ourselves, "from thee we come to thee we go." The days were long and full, but we still stayed up late talking excitedly, sharing our experiences.

The foundational theory was taught by Oscar himself, the Enneagram—a nine-pointed map of the psyche, and *trespasso*—sitting face-to-face, staring into the left eye of our partner. Physical exercises, mantra, and some theory were taught by a man they called Swami, short, wiry, intense and kind. He looked like an Indian *sadu*. Our experiences were intense and grew more intense in the fullness of time.

About three months into the training, a building was completed for us to do the work. We called it the *doyo*. A circle of rooms with a large roofless circular space in the center. There, we lined up to meet with Oscar individually and answer the Koan. When it was my turn, I sat in front of him and began looking into his left eye. At that point, he became a Chinese emperor with a long beard, brocade robe, and an ornate cap. Transfixed, I was seeing him from another time.

When the vision broke, he said, "Jane, I saw you as a Chinese princess. So beautiful."

My answer to the koan, "I am here."

"And where is here?"

I was stumped.

At night in the *doyo* under the stars, we sat on blankets, *zafu* and *zabutan* (meditation cushions and round pillows). We practiced *kinerythems* sitting under the stars, cross-legged, holding a palm-sized smooth stone in the right hand and moving it in a series of circles, elbow on the right knee, three circles, over and around the head, three circles and so on. All the while repeating inward *voluntar escuela silencio* (will, school, silence). I became the universe, the cosmos, a planet, circling the sun, a star, a constellation, endless space.

Each of us was to spend seven days alone in the Atacama Desert in a tiny hut. There were a few huts scattered a good distance from each other. But occasionally, I saw other trainees wandering along a ridge in the distance. The Atacama was where the astronauts trained for the moon landing. It was flanked by the Pacific Ocean. The exercise was to lie face down, forehead on our cupped hands and repeat internally, "I am in thy holy hands."

I had a secret affair with Martin, one of Oscar's Chileno students. We drove out to the desert after I snuck out of our room when Lyle was asleep. So much for a devoted girlfriend.

Days turned into weeks, weeks into months, as we came to the end. Our Sundays then were not *Pampas* but *Zikr*, dressing in our finest, bringing instruments, flute, drums, etc. and sitting in a circle in the *dojo*. We sang. We danced.

Zikr took on a new meaning later when we returned to the US. Oscar taught me the movements and taught Gordy and Christian the songs. I taught or passed the movements to the others while Gordy and Christian passed the music. I further sullied my lily-white reputation of myself by having a secret affair with Gordy.

When the training came to a close, Oscar announced that we as Arica Institute would move to New York City to teach what we had learned. Wait, what? We're not going back to Big Sur? This just came as a total shock to me. I had never lived in a city. Much less New York City.

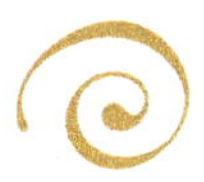

New York City
1971

New York was a shocking crime-filled city. That's how I saw and felt it. A woman was murdered on the street while onlookers watched in horror from their apartment windows and this was where we were planting our flag. Someone rented a big house in Bayville, New York, hours outside of the city. We settled there for a couple of weeks. There was a flu going around so lots of us were laid up. What a crash landing!

Lyle and Steve found a place on Central Park West, The Orwell House. It became a beehive of Aricans. Our apartment, a spacious two-bedroom overlooking Central Park would suffice for Steve, Linda and baby David, born in Chile, Lyle and me.

Once people got settled in New York, we were ready to start "The Mission." We, as close to enlightenment as one would hope, were charged with spreading the word, the Work, and saving humanity.

One of our monied members took out a full-page ad in *The New York Times*: THE MOSQUITO THAT BITES

THE IRON BULL, hoping that this koan (the mosquito being the ego and the bull being the essence) would spark interest, and attract people. A three-month training was offered. The phone number was posted, and that was it.

We set up a phone bank at the Essex House on Central Park South. People actually called. We rented a ballroom at Essex House and started off with a bang. It was the 70s, people were searching. Close to 300 people packed into the ballroom. We taught what we had learned: meditation, mantra, theory, the Enneagram, and more.

One evening, Adrienne knocked on our door. I answered. She looked like a ghost. "What's wrong?"

"Ramon is dead."

I thought she was sleepwalking and having a bad dream. But no, she and Gordy's little infant Ramon had died of meningitis in the night. She collapsed in the doorway. I picked her up in my arms. She was as light as a bundle of sticks. I took her into our bed and laid down with her spoon style. The paramedics had already taken Ramon's little body to the morgue. This brutal shock ricocheted through the school. Everything was falling apart.

My relationship with Lyle was done, not with a bang, but a whimper. We sat down face to face with a candle between us. *Om.* Then he announced that I was far too attached to him, which was in fact, true. I failed to recognize my part in it, playing the victim. Yet I had been sneaking off with Gordy for weeks.

As a group, we taught the three-month trainings. Oscar decided we should offer 40-day trainings instead. These spread to Boston, California, Florida, and elsewhere. Teaching houses sprang up everywhere, eventually trainings were offered in Europe. Arica became a buzz among spiritual seekers. I went to LA to teach the 40-day training, suffering with anorexia. My binging and purging were so extreme that I had worked myself into the place where I couldn't digest food. I was thin and jaundiced. Not a very good look for a spiritual teacher who is supposed to be enlightened. We had a beautiful beach house in Santa Monica and a teaching facility in Brentwood on Santa Monica Blvd. Oscar's secretary, Jenny Pereda, called from New York and announced that I was "circulated." Circulated means not only kicked out but shunned. I wasn't going anywhere. I just stayed, business as usual. Lyle sent me to one of his uncles who was a gastroenterologist. He asked me what I ate. I lied.

I was called back to New York to teach a six-week advanced training. Before it even started, I was "circulated" again for being controlling. Arica was a patriarchy and suggestions as to how to run things were frowned on. I suggested since people were pushing to get in that we should open the doors so someone wouldn't get crushed. Next thing I knew Steve and Camillo were coming to me holding a candle.

"Jane, we need to *Om* in."

"If you have something to say to me, you can say it right here to my face. I'm not gonna sit down and sanctify this shit!"

New students were pushing against the glass doors to get into the building.

Steve and Camillo, hiding behind faces of authority, chased me down the hallway, candle in hand. I stopped and turned around.

"Tell me what you have to tell me dammit!"

"OK, you're out," says Steve.

"So that wasn't so hard after all was it?" says I, holding back the tears with the outrage.

I was a zombie going down the escalator to the glass doors people were pushing. I pushed against the crowd amazed at my own strength, fueled by rage. I didn't care if they got in. I wasn't the guard dog anymore.

I hailed a cab back to The Orwell House, back to our old apartment. Everyone was moved out. There was no furniture, just the purple carpet and a rainbow painted on the wall. I lay down on the purple carpet and cried myself to sleep.

Bradley Marks arranged a job for me giving out grants in New York City from the Marks Company. Lost and alone, I showed up at nonprofits, schools mostly. I was given tours and treated like royalty. Of course, I sleepwalked through my days. It was September so the weather was changing, getting cold. I was wearing platform sandals.

Jake Brackman sent me a ticket back to LA and gave me a room in his newly rented house. An article was written in *Psychology Today*, reporting Arica as the cutting edge of higher consciousness. I returned to New York to share an apartment with my best friend Linda.

Arica Institute moved to our own space (thanks to a generous donor), at 24 W. 57th St. Students who completed the 40-day were offered the advance training. Meanwhile, besides enjoying our status as spiritual giants, we plunged into the 70s New York scene. Besides LSD and pot, cocaine had come into fashion.

I was running with Billy. He started up a lucrative drug dealing operation with friends from his home state Florida. I landed a job at *Saturday Night Live* as a masseuse to the talent. I spent days and evenings at Rockefeller Center. And of course I went to the show on Saturday night. Actually, there were two shows, one live show dress rehearsal at 10, and then the aired live show at 11:30. Local bars and restaurants competed to host a "cordial." Billy, my husband by then, and I attended, hobnobbing with the crew and talent. After that, the party moved to the Blues Bar in the Bowery, a private club owned by Dan Aykroyd and John Bellucci. The party raged on. People finally stumbled out of there in the harsh daylight of midday Sunday.

Sexually, we were changing partners. Seemed like everybody slept with everybody else. Couples were made, then dissolved, and more couples were made. Our monk-like demeanor dissolved.

Studio 54 beckoned and since my guy was a coke dealer, that red velvet barrier came down when we arrived. People packed into the bathrooms to snort coke. And they snorted it openly on the dance floor.

Billy and I took a trip to Hawaii to visit my folks. When we came back, I was pregnant, a stranger in a strange land. Everybody was rocking and rolling, but me. Arica was thriving. People were still signing up for 40-day trainings and advanced trainings. I ate, slept, and roller-skated around the city.

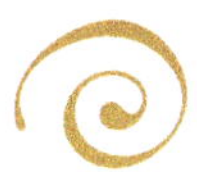

Escape from New York City to Hawaii and Florida
1980

My pregnancy turned out to be grievous and lonely. Cut off from the party scene in New York, I was isolated and solitary, relegated to pacing Central Park, crying and eating. The cigarettes my husband, Jim and Virginia smoked made me perpetually nauseous. Their ridiculous solution of me staying in the bedroom with the door closed, they claimed would protect me from the noxious smoke.

I took two trips out of New York while pregnant. My first, at four months, was to visit my parents in Hawaii. I should have stayed. My dear friend Zelita came from Kauai to visit for a week. On my parents' lanai, at a 500' elevation, we sat side by side, leaned our heads together and stared at the ocean. We took walks on Painted Church Road. We ate strawberry papaya, mangoes, ahi poke, laulau and kalua pig with rice and poi. Zelita had given birth to three babies and described childbirth as pushing a watermelon through one's nostril. Instead of being horrified, I laughed 'til I peed. Such a dear and loving friend Zelita. When I left the Big Island, I cried hard, foreshadowing the months to come.

In my eighth month, I flew to Key West to visit my cousin Dee Von for two weeks. She was a paralegal working for the local district attorney. Dee and her boyfriend Craig decided to spend the weekend on their sailboat. So grateful to be out of New York, I was content to stay behind in their rustic house, read, make art, swim, eat ice cream, and take naps. To provide me with a night out, she arranged for her boss to take me to dinner. Late Saturday afternoon, I ironed my maternity dress on a towel on the floor, faking an ironing board. I even put on makeup, wore the huge bra I was spilling out of, and squeezed my swollen feet into heels. When the boss arrived (whose name I don't remember, nor care to) I was hungry and uncomfortably put together.

All smile and style, looking like an aging blond surfer in an expensive aloha shirt, he opened the door of his shiny Cadillac for me. I appreciated being treated like a woman rather than someone who was suffering from the pitiful illness of pregnancy.

The restaurant was the most expensive in The Keys, he assured me. I received this information with indifference being no stranger to expensive restaurants. Yet this assured me the food would be good and the service prompt. I was famished as only a pregnant woman could be. People nodded in acknowledgement or glad-handed the DA as we walked in. The maître d' bowed and ushered us to a good table at the side of the room. Through a big picture window, the sunset faded into the sea.

When the waiter appeared, DA ordered a martini and turned to me. One jigger of liquor was allowed per day, according to my doctor. I ordered the same. Before the waiter withdrew, I asked about hors d'oeuvres.

"Tonight, we offer crab cakes, shrimp cocktail, Caprese salad, stuffed mushrooms and brie croquettes." I ordered everything. After all, I was hungry and there were two of us.

"Shall I serve them in courses?"

"No. Bring them as soon as they're ready," I retorted.

Drinks and appetizers appeared punctually. Mr. DA surveyed the array of food then met my eyes.

"So, Dee Von tells me you live in Manhattan?"

"That's right," I said through a mouthful of crab cake.

"What part of town?"

"Sixty-fifth and Third."

"Wow! That's a pretty swanky part of town. Your husband must have a great job!"

"Yes, he's a very successful drug smuggler."

He was nonchalant, even waving it off as I was discussing the weather. But, of course, I didn't.

"He is an importer."

While I was eating the hors d'oeuvres, he was drinking one martini after another. I hadn't noticed at first, being too interested in the spread, not in him. By the time the waiter brought yet another martini and removed the emptied glass, I realized he was getting lit as I was getting full.

DA summoned the waiter as I got started on the shrimp cocktail. He ordered rare filet mignon, baked potato, asparagus spears, and another martini. The waiter turned to me assuming I had enough food and asked if I would like another martini.

"No, but I'll have what he's having except medium rare on the steak," I said, staring into his face for a hint of judgement. I readied myself for a sarcastic comeback. "I'm carrying quintuplets, so eating for six."

Only a nod and, "very good Madam."

The judgments and condemnations were all piled up in my own head. I'm 5'2" and had been steadily climbing from my original weight of 115 pounds to 180 pounds and counting. My pregnancy, mournfully unhappy, had been endured by eating, stuffing down every fear, regret, and pain. Having been the movement, fitness and dance instructor extraordinaire, now I was just obese. I loathed my very own self, mocked my face in the mirror, and stared cruelly into my own visage.

Goddamn you stupid cow! What made you think this would work out? What made you think Billy would change? Why didn't you leave when he said it's either me or the kid? Why did you marry a man you didn't love and didn't love you? You are such a coward!

My twisted reverie broke as the waiter brought the main course. I noticed he too was unhappy. When our eyes met, I felt compassion for him that I couldn't feel for myself. He was inside his own world as he deftly carried, cleared, bowed, and nodded. I smiled. He smiled. He was elegant, slim, and angular. A Cuban with deep brown skin contrasted his glittering white teeth. How hadn't I noticed him? Inwardly, I apologized for begrudging him and imagined he forgave me.

My attention and contempt shifted to good old DA, now deeply in his cups as he regaled himself with courtroom triumphs. Seeming to have no idea that my attention was elsewhere, he expounded.

"They were sorry they hadn't agreed to settle out of court. I mean, I was cross-examining the shit out of him. Had him like a fish on a hook, just reeling him in."

"Hmm," was the best I could do, signaling the waiter.

"Can you please wrap this up for me?"

"Of course, Madam, shall I include the hors d'oeuvres as well?"

"Yes, thank you so much." Now an ally, a comrade in the struggle for survival.

"I'll have a nightcap and one for the little lady!" DA bellowed to the entire restaurant as if he were the main character in a play. He downed the remains of his martini and raised the empty glass toward me.

"No thank you. Not for me," wondering what kind of a drunk he was. Back slapping life of the party was my guess. He ordered a brandy and continued to recount his courtroom victories.

"I'm getting pretty tired," I said, feigning a yawn.

"Ok, little lady, let's move out" He snapped his fingers, then pretended to write on his palm. Our waiter jumped to attention and hurried for the check. Inebriated, DA fumbled for his wallet and slammed down his credit card.

The evening couldn't be over fast enough. As he stood to leave, I was willing to risk my life to get back and out of his presence.

As he wobbled to the car I asked, "Since you're a bit tipsy, could you possibly drive slow and carefully? I want to live to deliver this baby." I considered offering to drive, knowing it would be futile.

"Aw, honey, I'm nowhere near tipsy. After I chauffeur you home, I'll catch up with some buddies at my favorite watering hole. You're in good hands, believe me." I didn't. I thought about calling a taxi, but I didn't know the address. Bite the bullet. The restaurant was close, remembering the ride over.

He opened the door for me again as I reminded my-self I had seen my husband drive in this state. There was no need to make small talk as he continued the stream of braggadocio. When we arrived, he didn't make a move to exit.

"How 'bout I come in for a little spell? I happen to know where DeeVon and Craig keep their liquor." He leaned in, winking. I recoiled.

"Thanks for dinner. I'll let myself out," I said, as I opened my door before he could move.

"I hope you enjoy your friends," I waved from the front door.

Thank God! What an asshole. I stepped out of my shoes, peeled off my dress and bra, which had dug train track grooves around my ribcage. I found the over-sized tee shirt I slept in and laid down on my right-side welcoming sleep. A few familiar kicks to my liver reminded me I was a team. Sometimes powerful, this kick from her right foot illustrated where she was in space. Facing my right flank, the kicks, punches, and stretches endeared her to me. I knew she was a girl. In a dream, Jenny Pereda came to me with a newborn baby in her arms.

"Mira Jane, su niña preciosa!" Looking into her arms, I could see Lea's face just as it was. Wise almond eyes looked directly into my soul, high forehead, round cheeks, lips the Hawaiians call *cho cho* lips. Butterfly lips in Japanese, adopted in pidgin, the geisha heroine of the opera *Madame Butterfly*. Perfect. An old soul, we had met before.

When the kicking subsided, we slept, she nestled in her snug watery cradle. I settled with my left leg draped over two piled pillows, high enough that it cleared my belly. Another pillow for the side of my head and another between my arms. All quiet, all still at this late hour.

"HEY LITTLE LADY!" Banging sound at the bedroom window.

"Lemme in, I'm gonna find the little man in the boat!"

I shot to my feet and looked out the window. The streetlight shone along the side of the house and into the bedroom. It was him. already having managed to remove the screen, he banged again.

"C'mon, you know you want it! Lemme in!" Pushing up on the bottom of the window, he continued hollering. "Let's get into it baby! I'll find the little man in the boat and make you come! You'll thank me!"

Stumbling around the room, I found my weapon on the floor where I had left it. The heavy steam iron fit like a club in my right hand.

"I'll smash your face in with this iron, I swear to god," amazed at the volume of my voice.

"Awww, don't be like that. Lemme in. Open the window honey!"

His volume increased as he continued to bang on the window with his flat hand, the glass wobbled in the sill.

"STELLA!" he howled.

"Get the fuck out of here!" I ran to the front door, turned the lock, then through the bedroom, and bolted the lock on the back door. At the bedroom window, I looked for a lock at the top of the pane. Layers of paint rendered it useless. Yelling and banging continued. "You see what I have here? I can KILL you with this!" Sure of my word, I brandished the iron over my head. I had no doubt I could and would kill him with the force welling up inside. Protecting my baby, trembling with rage, I approached the window and slapped the palm of my left hand on the glass. "You hear me motherfucker!" He stepped back a few paces, fumbled with his fly and urinated on the lawn.

That's when I heard the sirens. Maybe I wouldn't have to kill him after all. More banging.

"It's the police, open the door." I went to the front door, turned the lock and opened it, visibly trembling.

"What's the problem ma'am?"

"It's around the side," I said still fuming. I joined them as they walked along the side of the house with their flashlights illuminating the pathetic scene. Attempting to zip his pants, mumbling and perplexed, he stumbled sideways, then looked up and welcomed the two officers with a wide grin.

"Hey fellas, it's a party!"

Clearly the cops knew him and addressed him by name as he finally secured the zipper.

"The neighbors called, said there was a disturbance out here."

"As in this asshole is trying to rape me!" I countered.

"Aww honey, you got it all wrong."

He outstretched his arms and took a step towards me. It was then I realized I was still holding the iron as I raised it above my head. Advancing toward him, one cop took his elbow.

"Time to go home sir, you're keeping the whole neighborhood up."

"Sir! Sir? This creep was trying to climb in the window and rape me!"

The cop responded in an attempt to soothe. "He just needs to go home and sleep it off."

"You mean you're not going to arrest him, put him in handcuffs, let him sleep it off in jail?"

"We'll take it from here. Looks like you're no worse for the wear."

It dawned on me. This was their boss's boss who wouldn't even get a slap on the wrist. There was no one to do the slapping. They've probably dealt with this sort of thing many times.

"And what if he comes back?"

"He won't ma'am. We'll take his keys."

Wow, clearly they're practiced in these events.

"I promise you if he does come back, I WILL KILL HIM! I MEAN IT."

"Ok, ok, you mean it," he says condescendingly.

"I can't fucking believe this!"

"No need for vulgar language ma'am."

"Fuck you and the DA too."

"Can I have your keys sir?"

Now mumbling to himself, he reached in his pocket, held out his keys then bent forward and vomited on his shoes. I watched as one of the cops got into the Cadillac, the other got into the squad car with DA in the passenger seat and drove off.

A young studious looking woman with glasses and curly hair walked quietly from the back of the house.

"Hello?" she said in a soft voice. "I'm the one who called the police. Are you alright? I rent the back house. Are you ok?" I leaned into her concern.

"I don't know. I guess so." Shoulders slumping forward, defeated, I broke down crying.

"My gosh, no telling what would've happened if the cops hadn't come."

"I would've killed him is what would've happened. I would've laid that bastard out," I said, still trembling, surging adrenaline. "Thank you so much for calling the police."

"Can I make you a cup of tea? Maybe it will calm you?" she offered.

"Yeah sure, that would be good. "I'm still upset. Thanks."

"My bungalow is back here."

In the five days I had been there, I hadn't noticed the miniature house, so close to the back door, thinking I could've sought out her company while Dee was at work for the asshole DA. She opened the front door, the only door. The kitchen, bedroom, and sitting room were all one little room.

"Where do you work?" I asked without curiosity or interest, just needing to connect.

"I'm a teacher, third grade." This caught my attention. No wonder her gentle demeanor.

"I bet you're good." She filled the red enamel teapot and put it on the gas burner. Her antique stove looked like a child's toy, similar to the little one I had in Big Sur when I lived in the maid's quarters.

"Thank you. It's a challenge, like herding cats."

Still wracked with anxiety, I soothed myself with a deep full breath, then another and another. She put two porcelain cups, white with pink roses, on saucers. Reminiscent of a grandmother's china, they made a soft clinking sound as she lifted them from the counter and placed them on the table. Reaching to the top shelf, she retrieved a box.

"Constant Comment, ok?"

"Perfect."

She ceremoniously put in the bags, being mindful to drape the strings outside the cups close to the handles. Turning to the sink, she picked up the matching sugar bowl with handles on either side. Sitting on the only other chair, she raised her head and smiled. Her features were delicate, eyes dark, nose pointed, lips thin, hair short with tight curls.

"Am I keeping you up?" I asked, reaching for the sugar bowl. "It's so late."

"Oh no, it's Saturday night. I've been having a restful day. I'll have another one tomorrow."

We sipped, listening to the nocturnal chorus of cicadas, crickets, katydids, and grasshoppers. There we were, two little girls in our pajamas having a tea party at two in the morning. Me in my XXL tie dye T-shirt and she in white cotton pajama pants and a white "wife beater." There's got to be a less brutal name for those. They always reminded me of Brando standing under the balcony yelling STELLA! Now I have to remember, against my will, the DA earlier in the evening.

"I'm Jane," I offered, "Dee Von's cousin." Better late than never with the intro. I guess.

"I'm Nancy." She smiled again.

Nancy, my guardian angel, all in white, swooped to my rescue, preventing me from committing bloody homicide. As I finished my tea, a weighted blanket of fatigue spread over me. I put my hands on the table to push myself up. It was a flimsy card table covered with a flowered cloth. It wouldn't hold my weight, so I pushed down my legs to stand, putting my palms on my lower back.

"You helped me so much tonight. I really appreciate you. Honestly."

"I think any decent person would've done the same thing," she said.

"Maybe, but you're the decent person who did and I'm grateful. I really think, hope, I can sleep in peace. How 'bout you Nancy?"

"Yes, I'm ready for a good sleep. Goodnight Jane. It was good to meet you, even in this terrifying circumstance."

"Good to meet you too, Nancy. I'll never forget your kindness to me and my baby."

I plodded around the house to the front door, locked it, and laid down with all the pillows. The kicking resumed on my right. I wrapped my arms around my bulbous belly, grateful she was there, joined to me, beating my blood with her heart, safe. I vowed to always keep her that way and drifted to sleep.

The next morning, I called the airlines and bumped up my return flight a week and called Greyhound to reserve a seat on the bus for Miami. No reservation needed. It would take four hours twenty minutes with two stops. First bus was 4 a.m. My flight was noon. I'd take the 6 a.m. Monday. Last time I rode a Greyhound was when Zelita and I got out of prison—Pennsylvania to Salt Lake City, Utah. I was with her though; it made the trip bearable. Now I'd be alone.

No, I'd be with my precious child. She deserves safety, sanity, and calm. I need to provide that. I made a vow to give her these things, plus the most important thing, unconditional love. She is the dependent, I am the mother. These obvious facts sank deeply into my psyche in that moment. I was thinking like a strong woman. My women ancestors, hard as stones, came from Ireland with their babies. My great-grandmother had twelve children. I could and would do this.

I bathed, washed my hair, rubbed my belly with coconut butter, peeled an orange and ate it, section by section. Summer had arrived in The Keys, bright and blazing hot. I was already glazed with sweat. I hadn't yet found my way to the ocean and felt too hot to search. I'd ask Nancy.

Careful to avoid the urine and vomit in the little side yard, I stepped on the beige mat with a bright red *Welcome* flanked with coconut palms. And timidly knocked.

"Nancy are you awake?" I heard footsteps, then a creek of the heavy wood door. This little bungalow must've been built in the thirties, like the front house.

"Good morning, Jane. How did you sleep last night?"

"Oh, my goodness! Did I wake you?" I noticed she was still in her white T-shirt and pants.

"Oh no, I've been up for hours. Have you had breakfast? Want coffee? Come in, please." The same sweet smile lit up her face. Her dark eyes sparkled. She was genuinely happy to see me and I her.

"Only if I'm not interrupting anything. I just came back to ask which way is the beach?"

"I'd love to walk you there, it's not far. Only if you'll have breakfast with me, or at least a cup of coffee." The wall clock signaled 9:20. I hadn't had coffee or anything but an orange.

We had our coffee in the same china cups. It was already made in a French press and hot. It was a new day. I would offer myself to mother ocean. Rest in her womb for the day.

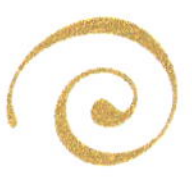

Lea's Birth
New York City
1980

June 1980, New York City, I had reached the ninth month of pregnancy. It was hell. I looked nothing like the beatific pregnant goddesses I had known in Big Sur. Golden beauties, slim in limbs, full bellies, sun drenched, golden, languishing in the Esalen baths. Fat had taken over my thighs, ankles, arms, face and neck. My hair hung in greasy strings. The famous "glow" women are supposed to have was lost to me. In its place, a slick veneer of sweat.

My exciting job as masseuse for *Saturday Night Live* had come to a halt when my bulbous belly began to bump against my clients like a medicine ball. Also, I couldn't see my hands. I stopped going to the cordials and blues bar after the shows, couldn't stay up all night. Yet, for my husband, the party raged on. He was never home nights, slept most of the day. I fended for myself, a stranger in a strange land. I had one last night at Studio 54 in a silk batik dress I designed. Miserable as a dancing hippo in Walt Disney's *Fantasia*.

At term, labor kicked in. Midnight, I called my husband's girlfriend's apartment. No one would admit to the coupling, but I had lost my post as number one fuck bunny, what with being pregnant and enormous. She answered. I announced I was in labor, and he might want to come home. Turned out to be false labor and I was admonished for interrupting his "work." I was married to the neighborhood drug dealer. His girl, the 18-year-old sister of his partner.

My mother flew in from Hawaii on a Friday morning. She walked past me at the gate having failed to recognize her immense daughter.

"Mom, I feel like I'm getting my period, how can that be?" I said, while shopping at D'Agostinos Grocery.

"You're in labor honey,"

"Really? Labor is like cramps?"

"Yes, in the beginning."

Early labor seemed doable. The doctor told me to hang around home until the pains were five minutes apart, then call her. I stayed up with Mom while she scared the crap out of me with tales of her own six deliveries. I slept off and on Friday night turning from side to side, rearranging pillows, peeing every fifteen minutes. Saturday morning came with the usual karate chop to my liver. The cramps, now nauseatingly intense. I spent the day groaning, getting in and out of the shower, pacing. Saturday night, more of the same. Mom and my husband amused themselves timing my contractions 'til he had to go out, and she to bed. I followed her into the massage room.

"Ok Mom, I'll wake you when it's time to go to the hospital."

"Oh no honey, I won't be going along with you to the hospital."

"Why not?" I moaned.

"Sweetie, a mother is not meant to watch her daughter suffer so much," she said in her most pseudo-soothing voice.

"Pleeeeeze come," I whimpered.

"I'll be right here when you get home. I'll change the baby when it wakes and bring it to you to nurse."

I stood there as another earth-shattering contraction took over my body. Where was the soft guitar? The candle glow? The choir of hippie angels singing *Oms*? Where was the birthing tent? The sacred water? Questions to no one. I stood in the shower, weeping in pain.

My rogue husband came home around 3 a.m.

"Wake me when you're ready to go to the hospital."

I had gone unaccompanied to Lamaze classes, shopping for baby supplies and doctors. What made me think he would deal himself in now? By 4:15 a.m., the contractions were spaced in the required order. I called my doctor apologizing for the time.

"Meet me at the hospital."

Time to wake the man of the house who was conscious enough to say, "I'll call for a car."

"But we have a car," I squeaked, tears brimming.

"I will have to drive though."

I was supposed to see the logic there. He would be inconvenienced. Finally, I snapped.

"Fuck you! I'll walk to the hospital. Go back to sleep."

After all we were on 86th Street. Lennox Hill Hospital was only eleven blocks down Lexington. Sunday pre-dawn, I set out, fueled by burning rage with no packed bag, no identification. I averaged one contraction per block. Power waddling as they increased their force. Iron storefront gates were all pulled shut. I curled my fingers on the highest bars and suspended myself for the duration of the contraction like a primate in the zoo. Genius method to get the pressure off my guts. Block six, my husband pulled up in the car.

"Get in," he barked.

"Fuck you, asshole."

"Get in the goddam car!"

"Kiss my ass!" I spat as I marched onward to block seven.

An off-duty NYPD officer in his black and white appeared.

"Is this man bothering you ma'am?"

"He's bothering the shit out of me!"

Contraction struck. I hung panting. As soon as it quit, I pressed on.

"She's my wife and she's in labor," husband tells cop.

"He is still bothering the shit out of me," I yelled.

"Ma'am, can I give you a ride to the hospital?" Cop asks.

I can't imagine folding myself in half, enjoying his concern.

"Can't sit down," I grunt.

"How 'bout I follow along to make sure you get there safely?"

"Ok," I sputter hanging somewhere in block eight.

The strange parade continued on to Lennox Hill Hospital.

"I'm going to park the car," husband announced. I scowled.

At the desk I leaned in for another vice-grip contraction. A wheelchair pushed up behind me.

"I can't sit down!"

Plop. The nurse pushed me into the chair. "I'm going to check you," she said shoving her hand into my vagina. Something flashed like a crochet hook and splush—my water.

I stood up on impulse as water flooded my legs.

"What the!?" I whimpered, invaded.

"Oh, I had to break your water, doctor's orders," the nurse explained briskly.

Where am I? I asked myself. What the fuck? I was being prodded and poked, wheeled to a bed, blood pressure, IV fluids, baby heart monitor. As the nightmare ramped up its intensity, a nurse came in looking like Marilyn Monroe. An angel sent from heaven, soothing tone, soft hands, deep blue eyes and kind smile.

"My name is Joanne. I'll be your nurse. Is there any-thing I can do for you?" she murmured.

"Will you please stay with me?" I pleaded.

"Of course, sweetie, I'm your nurse. I have no other duties but to care for you, help you get this baby born."

I surrendered to the bed, the hospital, the moment. The doctor came in, no nonsense New York Woman, jet black hair perfectly coiffed, pearls.

"Shall I give you a spinal? Have you had enough of this pain?"

"I want to deliver naturally, remember we talked."

"In my book there's no such thing. I can do a spinal and a C-section right now. You can even watch!" she chirped.

"Doesn't sound like..." Oooooh another contraction. Eyes rolled back, facial skin stretched into a grimace, head lurched forward, chin to chest.

"I'll give you some time," she said as she breezed out. I had been squeezing Joanne's hand until it turned white.

"Sorry," I said as I released her. "I almost squeezed your hand off."

"You'll have to squeeze a whole lot harder to do that. Being with a birthing woman is my favorite thing."

She meant it. I exhaled, trusting Joanne, submit-ting as she spooned ice chips, sponged my forehead, plumped pillows, massaged my neck and feet.

The doctor returned, all business.

"I'm thinking C-section, and everybody goes home," she said.

I snapped for the second time that day. "Am I in trouble? What's your reason to cut me open?"

"No, not just now. but you have been in labor since Friday afternoon. You've been in hard labor since Saturday. It's 7:30 Sunday morning. I'm gonna be concerned for you and the baby," she explained

"And exactly when will you actually be concerned?" Pant, wheeze.

"If you haven't gone into transition by 9, I will be officially concerned."

"OK, get out and don't come back until 9!" I order.

"Good for you Jane," Joanne whispers. "Way to take charge of your own labor."

"It's gonna look weird but I need to roll onto my belly next contraction. Need to push the baby's head into the birth canal with both my hands, don't freak," I said.

"All right let's go. It's your body, you know how to do this thing," Joanne says.

For the next 90 minutes, with every contraction, I splayed on my stomach, cheek jammed in the mattress, rooting into my belly with both hands. Like a wild animal I snorted, growled and panted. Finally, I felt the baby's head slide into the birth canal. At exactly 9, Doc filled her promise as she opened the door.

"Good job Mama!" She exclaimed. "You are definitely in transition. Now let's get you into the delivery room and get that girl out of there."

"Girl? How do you know it's a girl?" I ask.

"Only a girl would put her mama through such hell," she joked.

That's when I remembered she had a little daughter. I remembered the dream I had at month four. My friend Jenny presented me with my newborn girl. I remember my husband waving off the dream, bent on a boy.

"Can't wait to teach my son to play baseball."

"Girls play baseball too."

Doc asked Joanne. "Didn't your shift end hours ago?"

"I can't go home, I have to meet this amazing woman's baby," she winked.

"Ok you can finally push girl, I know you want to," Doc said.

"You can do this Jane," Joanne chimed in as I squeezed the hand I had been holding all this time.

Then on my back, I clutched one of my feet in each hand and pushed the arches of my feet into my forehead, Aztec birthing goddess style. Joanne and my husband pushed my shoulders forward. I didn't scream. One last long hard push and whoosh. No crying, all quiet.

"She's beautiful," says Doc. as she hands her off to Joanne.

"Let me see," I say, arms outstretched.

"First the placenta, then you can have her. One two three—push!"

Another whoosh. A perfect peach colored girl with orange hair was placed carefully on my chest. Tears streamed. She pushed her tiny new hands into my sternum; her head and shoulders came up like a baby sphinx. Head wobbling, she looked into each face circled around my head, the anesthesiologist, my husband, Joanne, then me. Suddenly, she lost control of her perfectly shaped head. Her pointy chin came down on my breastbone. She cried. Not like a baby but like an angry tiger. Again, she pushed herself up to roar in my face. A mighty roar that blew back my hair making me feel small and helpless. Put her back, I hear myself think, joking only to me.

Home from the hospital, I was writhing in pain from the episiotomy. Billy offered to take Lea's birth certificate to the city registry. Fine with me. One problem—I insisted, after much argument, that we spell Lea's name the Hawaiian way, Lia. I didn't find out 'til years later that he chose Lea. Yet one more betrayal to add to a long list!

I was an anxious, exhausted, depressed, and fearfully manic new mother. Lea, now three months old, was equally miserable and colicky.

My husband hadn't taken to new fatherhood. He stayed out until two or three in the morning and slept until the afternoon. I was convinced he was having an affair, though he denied it vehemently.

The city was a hell hole in summer, hot, sticky, humid, and the air was foul. Anyone with means left town. We had means, shoeboxes full of money, it was doled out to me to cover my needs. I needed to get out, left New York, either nestled her down to sleep in her bassinet or stare wide eyed out the rear window as I held her over my shoulder. She nursed and burped like other babies and only fussed when she needed to be changed.

We went to Southampton with Adrienne to visit my ex-boyfriend, Lyle and my best friend Linda. In a rented house above the ocean surrounded by trees, their affair had become serious. I would forfeit my dignity for a few days out of the sweltering city. The air, the trees, and the ocean made me feel so peaceful and free, I momentarily relinquished my resentment and jealousy. Early the next morning, after nursing, we stepped out into the misty quiet. Lea, content in the yellow seersucker snuggly slept next to my heart, perfect peach head just under my chin. A hammock, strung between two massive pine trees beckoned. Leaning cautiously on the edge, I hoisted up my backside, laid down, kept my right foot on the ground and rocked. Looking skyward, the pines created patterns of branches and needles against the sky. This was the calmest I'd been in a very long time. A rhythmic creaking sound from the ropes securing the hammock encouraged a morning nap. Creek, creek, creek, and SNAP! The rope at my feet broke, crashing my massive postpartum body on the hard ground. My sacrum made contact first, then my back. Lea, jolted to rigid attention, screamed urgently. Lying on the ground, both hands patting and stroking her little back, I silently wept, hoping someone would come to our aid. With every wail, Lea squeezed the air from her lungs, followed by an interminable pause 'til the next inhale. Panic set in.

"Help, help, help!" I bellowed louder with each plea. Adrienne came first, still shrouded with sleep, matted hair and pajamas.

"Oh babe! What happened?" She asked, although the evidence was clearly laid out.

"Fell."

"Do you think you can get up?"

"No, leave us. No, don't leave us!"

"Of course not! Should I call an ambulance?"

"No."

"What should I do?"

"Take the baby." With both arms around Lea, I rolled partially on my side. Searing pain stabbed my sacrum and back. Adrienne undid the straps of the snuggly, stepped over me and lifted her out. I got on all fours, carefully stood up and checked if anything was broken. I said to myself, I'm in one piece, I'm whole.

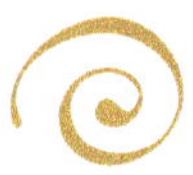

Swimming with Dolphins
Hawaii

1981

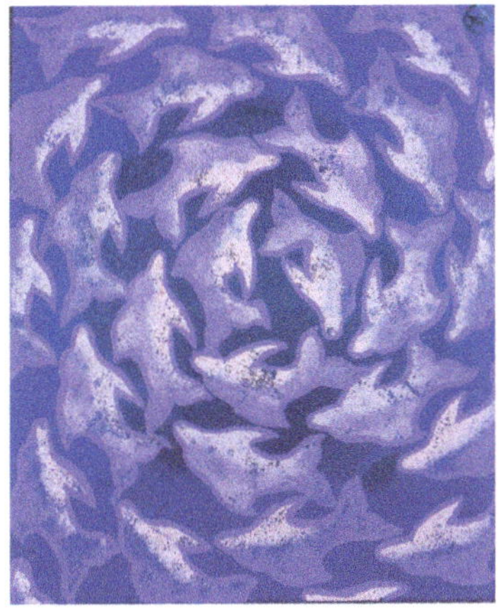

A Pod of Dolphins

Swimming with the dolphins of Kealakekua Bay was a way of life. First, I'd put Lea on the school bus at 7:15. Though she could easily walk, I drove her to the bottom of the mango farm driveway. Then I wound down past the plumeria farm's pungent perfume and warm fragrance from the coffee farm roasters. Painted Church Road, Middle Keei Road, Napoopoo Road, and to the

Bay. At 7:30 I parked under the banyon tree with my fins, mask and snorkel, gloves and towel. I walked to the sea wall to look for dolphins, check out the waves, and take in the morning.

Napoopoo Beach is no idyllic white sand beach, it's rocks. A pile of rocks. The east side of the bay is a massive cliff carved sheer by earthquakes. The bare strata reveal lava tubes where the Alii (Hawaiian royalty) buried their dead.

On the north side of the bay stands Captain Cook's Monument, a white spire on a cement platform. Erected by the British in 1778, it marks the spot Cook landed and eventually fell.

The Hawaiians mistook Cook for the god Lono, God of the Harvest. Lono's color is white, like the sun. So, with the white sails and the white skin and all, the assumption was made and stayed. The so-called discoverer of the islands didn't have the humility to admit he was no god, just a sailor, and pride came before the fall.

Navigating the smooth, slick boulders and rocks into the water is a tricky proposition. Fins and mask in hand, I'd gingerly make my way to shore, then gauge the rhythm and size of the waves before making the plunge.

If there were spinner dolphins anywhere near, I'd hear the high-pitched ringing peals and clicks of their conversation. This would be my course, toward the sounds until I caught up with the pod.

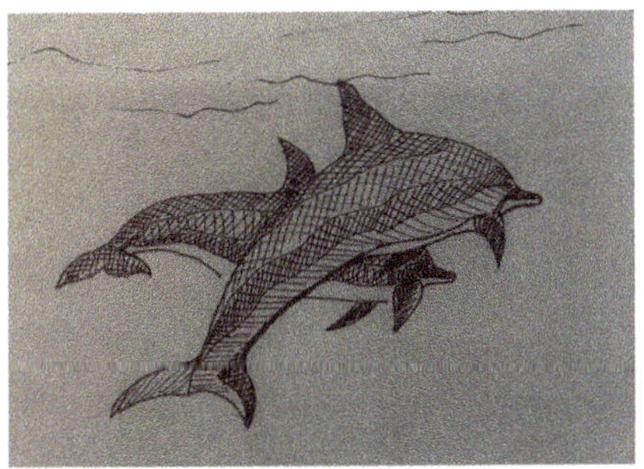

Dolphins

At night they feed way out on the Pacific Shelf, hunting in packs, chasing down their prey up to 25 miles per hour. Morning is their time to rest, socialize and sexualize. Mothers nurse their young, roughneck teenagers nip at each other, slap their flukes on the surface, dive deep and race up for high twisting somersaults. Males swim upside down under females with their dagger penises unsheathed. If the female accepts him, she stays her course. If not, she shifts one degree and the male moves on.

Sleeping dolphin style means closing one eye shutting down half the brain. This requires watchfulness on the surrounding pod members to watch over the vulnerable sleeper.

For years, I doggedly chased dolphins. I'd catch up, swim hard to keep up.

Until one night I had a dream. I walked into my bedroom to find a dolphin sleeping in my bed. I told him I loved him, but he was sleeping. I said it louder. He slept. I jarred him with my hand. "Wake up, I love you!" Still nothing. My conscience woke before me that morning, the morning I decided to never chase dolphins again.

From then on, I followed my conscience toward Cooks Monument. If the pod or any of its members wanted to join me, I would welcome them. If not, I swam to the monument and back.

Once, setting out for a lonely swim to the monument, convinced there would be no encounters, I put my head down to face the blackness below. The bay is not only a mile wide but a mile deep. It is flanked by some of the most beautiful reefs in the world, but the inky center evokes fear of the unknown. Seemingly out of nowhere a huge male spinner appeared at my left side. My first reaction was a shock of fear, mistaking him for a shark. I knew better but when you tell yourself don't think about sharks, it's the first thing you think about. We made eye contact. I imagined he sensed my relief, my gratitude. I rolled onto my right side, he on his left. I nodded my head as I've seen them do a thousand times. He nodded his head. I dove. He dove. I swam on the surface. He did too. I was full of pleasure and happiness. He was too as evidenced by his unsheathed penis. Male dolphins don't become erect when aroused. Their penises don't engorge with blood. They can present them from a fold in their lower body at will. He swam rolling side to side, pleasuring himself. I laughed into my snorkel. He never left my left side. When we reached the monument, I said goodbye and thank you with keening squeals and cried into my mask.

I got out, shed my gear and sat down on the warm cement platform. Across the bay, the sheer cliffs and sparkling ocean hummed with beauty. The palm trees, the green carpet up the flank of Mauna Loa Mountain, seemed to breathe. I thanked whatever great mysterious force had blessed me with this experience.

Rested, I grabbed my gear and jumped into the water. There he was, waiting to escort me back to Napoopoo. My protector, my friend.

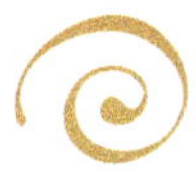

Humpback in the Bay
Hawaii
1987

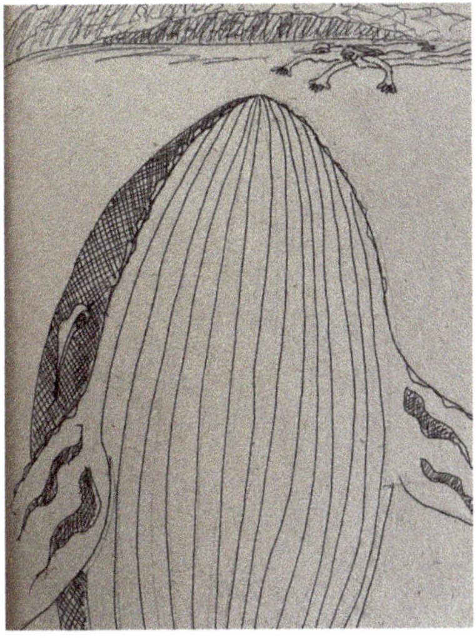

Humpback

Humpback songs vibrate through your whole body if you're lucky enough to be in the same water at the same time. The high pinging falsetto shakes your spine and thrills the nervous system. The low booming baritone goes to your guts, orgasmic.

Christine and I had been searching for two days. We watched them breech and heard them sing both mornings. We swam from one side of the bay to the other hoping to see one face to face. No luck. We assumed there was at least one mother and calf by the breaching flukes we spotted. Always too far away to catch up, not that we didn't try.

On our third morning, we agreed to just swim to Captain Cook's Monument. We considered ourselves lucky to have been bathed in holy whale song for two long mornings. Resolute, we set off, no spinner dolphins, no whale songs. The bay was glassy and still. Without the circus thrills of cetaceans, the mile swim is long.

After a short rest, the way back from the monument was just as monotonous. Then I saw it. A downed airplane with its nose just beneath the surface? Something huge in the distance. All the sights I had seen in deep water rolled through my memory like the pictures in slot machines, each rejected out of hand. Finally, the three pictures lined up and clunked into place. Vertical humpback whale. It's snout one yard from the surface. An immense angel, pectoral fins embracing and being embraced by the sea. Time slowed to a crawl. I unfolded from the tight ball I had coiled into. We continued to swim into the whale's neighborhood, her block, next door, front yard, front door. Eyeball the size of my head told me I was under its microscope and in its sonar view. I was acknowledged as part of her and regarded her with reverence. All part of one watery world. Christine reeled in excitement. She motioned to the surface with her thumb.

"What?"

"Should we go closer? Should we try to touch?"

"Chris, we should go back down."

The eye is surveying us both. Someone is pulling on the leg hole of my suit.

"What should we do?"

"We should savor this experience. We are the only people in the universe having it."

In as long as it took to make that statement, the whale had gone horizontal and moved across our view like a slow train. Whale, whale, whale, whale. We instinctively came to the surface. Its giant fluke pushed a 30-foot wall of water above us. A waterfall pounded down in front of us.

I looked over at Christine, mouth gaping, snorkel mouthpiece hanging to the side. We screamed joy, hugged, laughed and choked.

"We gotta settle down or we're gonna drown."

A few more hugs, pumping fins as to not go under. Then back to shore.

The experience was so vivid that when my head hit the pillow, I summoned it up again. As Elton John sang, "how wonderful life is with you in the world."

David's Departure
Hawaii
1981

Monica was a nurse at Kona Hospital. This was her last day on the Big Island. It was almost over. She'd move back to the mainland the next day. She was leaving the going away party that the hospital staff had thrown. She could easily have gone back to Kailua town, but she was coming to the mango farm to spend the night. Everything she had was packed in her car. She was looking forward to waking up in the middle of a mango orchard and gazing at the Pacific as Honaunau came to life.

I was fast asleep. It was late. I didn't hear her come in, but I did hear the phone ring, thinking someone forgot the time difference. "Hello?" I heard mumbling then the floor creak as she came down the hall. It was best she had answered the phone.

"Jane, you need to take this."

"Who is it?"

"The police."

This got my attention and out of bed. I wracked my brain trying to think of any laws I had broken. None since sobriety. That's where I met Monica. It had been a couple years then. Long enough for us to become friends for life.

"Hello?"

"Is this Jane Watkins?"

"Yes," I said, stomach tightening.

"Is David Watkins your brother?"

My voice drew out a long shaky, "Yeeesss?"

"Your brother has been involved in a accident on Kuakini Highway."

My heart began to pound against the inside of my sternum. Speeding up as it pounded. My head felt light as I gripped the phone. My body began to tremble. I realized I was holding my breath. Sucking in a gulp of air, on the exhale out came, "Is he dead?"

David rode his bike everywhere, to town, which was 12 miles, and back. He refused to wear a helmet and had only reflective lights front and back. People would tell me in the grocery store, on the beach, or at canoe races, "Eh I almos buss up your bruddah on Mamalahoa goine sout. Why he no mo light?"

"I beg him to get a helmet and lights. He neva listen." When I talked with locals, I immediately switched to pidgin, knee jerk.

"Is he dead?" I asked in a trembling voice. No answer.

"Is he dead?" Now screaming.

"I'm sorry ma'am, we cannot give that information on the phone."

"IS HE DEAD? IS HE DEAD?" Monica was still standing by my side. She put her hand on my back between my shoulder blades.

"So, he's dead then."

"I'm sorry ma'am, we cannot. . ."

I cut him off. "Have you called my parents?"

"Mrs. Watkins, you are the first one we called. The paramedic is in Keoua. He knows you. He knows you have a brother on the island."

"What should I do now?" I plead.

"Maybe call your parents."

I didn't know how or when to hang up the phone. I was still holding it in a vice grip to my ear, trying to stop it from shaking. Silence except for the hollow sound coming from the phone, like I was holding a big conch shell up to my ear. "Ok, I'm hanging up now," I said, breaking the emptiness. "I'm going to hang up." Putting down the receiver, I turned to Monica. My body was freezing cold from the inside out. I was shivering, my jaw shaking.

"David is dead," I announced. "He wouldn't tell me, but I know it."

"Oh no! Oh my god, Jane. What happened?"

Shaking all over, I didn't respond to her question.

"Monica I'm really cold. It's in my bones." Shoulders drawn up, arms folded.

"Let's put you in a warm shower," Monica said in a soothing voice. She took me by my quivering hand and let me out the screen door. The outside shower was the one we used when we came home from the beach or after picking mangoes sweaty from the relentless Hawaiian sun, or after canoe practice.

"Let me get it warm for you first." I stood naked with my arms around my body, shaking uncontrollably.

"Ok, it's ready for you, honey." Monica spoke in a sing-song gentle voice as if speaking to a traumatized child. I stepped up on the wooden planks and all the way into the warm water. What a relief. I let it run over my whole head, down my face, my chattering jaw, my stiffened shoulders, my clenched chest and stomach. I turned and let it melt my back, my bones.

"Monica, can we make it a little hotter?"

"Sure dear, but just a bit. It's pretty hot already."

As I stood under the water, I gave myself to the warmth. Gave in to the melting sensation from head to toe, like a candle. The heat seeped into my center, my bone marrow. My guts got warm and relaxed.

"Is this a dream or is it real?" I sprinted out of the shower barefoot and naked, uphill to David's trailer.

"DAVID! DAVID! DAVID!" He would be home. This was a bad nightmare. Monica ran after me.

"Jane stop! Come back here! You're tearing up your feet on the lava rocks!" Lava rocks. It's real. My shoulders slumped forward into sobs. Monica walked up gingerly in her flip flops to walk me down. I couldn't feel my feet. We went slowly down to the carport.

Nausea swept from my core making its way to my throat. I leaned over as vomit shot from me to the cement with such force that it splashed back into my face. For the second time that evening, Monica put her gentle hand on my back.

"You're in shock Janie girl. You're in shock."

Then the cold came back, crawling up my spine, working its way to my core, shaking my jaw.

"Let's get you back into the shower again." It was still running, still warm.

"I'm in shock? This is real?"

"Yes, you're in shock. Breathe deep and slow. Don't pant. One, two, three, four. Out two, three, four. Soft, slow, gentle soothing breath."

My breath slowed like it does in scuba diving. My body began to cool like the ocean. I stayed safe in my breath, which took me high into the night skies, high as a distant star. I watched, detached, as my tiny insignificant self kept writhing, vomiting, into and out of the shower screaming, keening. Monica by my side. I watched myself, down on the carport. Impassive, I took another smooth breath. This breath shot me back to earth to a tiny island in the Pacific. I was in the shower. The star was in my head now. Between my eyebrows it pulsed and sparkled. It looked out to the world through my own eyes.

"Monica, can you bring me that beach towel from the clothesline? I've got to dry off and get dressed, call my folks."

"Be happy, my dear." Monica dried my body. We went inside the back door and to the bathroom. "Keep this towel around you while I dry your hair." She was so much taller than me. She had the same square jaw. Her blond hair feathered away from her head.

"I love you, Monica."

"I love you too Janie girl." She peered into my eyes. Hers were watery green like the foamy edge of the surf.

"What do you want to wear?"

"I'll get it Monica. You better change. You're pretty wet." I went into the bedroom for a clean T-shirt and a pair of old sweatpants. When I came back into the kitchen, Monica was sitting at the table, quiet with her hands folded in front of her.

"I've got to call Mom and Dad, and I know the number by heart, but I can't remember." Monica suggested we look in the phone book.

"Good idea!" My mind was tired. My whole being drained. Monica recited the number while I dialed. I was starting to shake. Back to my breath I was able to slow it, calm it, feel its warmth. The star reappeared, brought back by my breath.

"Hello?" Mom said. Her voice sounded high-pitched, worried.

"Sorry to call so late Mom. Can you sit down? Are you sitting down?"

"I haven't stood up. Your dad and I were asleep. I'm sitting on the bed. What is it Jane? What's wrong?" Her voice raised another octave. "Tell me, tell me Jane!"

"Mom, David has been in an accident on Kuakini. His bike was hit and knocked off the road. His head struck the lava. He died instantly. We need to go to Kona hospital and identify the body."

I was able to recount the event because I saw it unfold in front of me as I said the words. It felt as though someone was speaking through me. My voice was eerily calm, measured. My tone was loving.

"No," was all she said.

"Monica is here with me, we will meet you and Dad at Kona Hospital, ok?"

"NO. NO. NO. NO." I hear my dad's voice. "What is it Vaye?" I hear the fear in his voice. Mom hung up the phone. She will tell Dad. They will be there. More knowing inside me, still witnessed by the star.

"We gotta meet my folks at Kona Hospital. Will you drive my car?" Her car was piled to the gills with suitcases and duffle bags. Her friend Sissy had bought it from her and Monica would pick her up on her way tomorrow.

"Of course." I got into the passenger seat and rolled down the window in preparation for more vomiting.

"Wait. I've got to get a sweatshirt."

I ran to my bedroom letting the screen door slam. Grabbed my blue sweatshirt, turned around, rushed through the door and let it slam again. The night was cloudless, so inky black that it made the stars more luminous. No moon. Where was the moon? I looked up to check for my star. Yes. There she was. Watching everything. Striking the balance. Not hot, not cold. Not bad, not good. Not inside, not outside. Not happy, not sad. Only witnessing. Monica started my trusty old white Toyota. I always kept the keys in it, so they'd never get lost.

We wound down the mango farm road. Left on Painted Church Road. Past the big avocado tree on the Mauka side. Left on City of Refuge Road. Left at Mamalahoa Highway. We snaked our way on the flank of Mauna Loa, long mountain, Goddess Pele's Mountain. Honaunau School on the Mauka side.

"Oh my God! Lia! We left her home by herself!" Cold fear and panic ripped into my guts.

"No Janie, she is on the mainland visiting her dad," Monica reminded me.

I calm my breath again. Soft, slow, calm and gentle breath. I needed to vomit but I did it quickly and efficiently. When I was on the escort boat in a race and the gas fumes made me sick, I just leaned over the side and puked. No one was the wiser.

The huge old jacaranda tree at the corner marks Hospital Road. Breathe. The star was watching evenly, dispassionate. We pulled into the lower parking lot. Mom stopped pacing when she saw us drive in. She started walking towards the car. I hardly recognized her. She had a wild, angry look on her face. I approached her expecting to fold her into my arms. She was rigid as a plank. I put my arms around her rigid body. She was unresponsive. I squeezed trying to press her into me, me into her. I started to pat her back like she does all her children and grandchildren. Her arms stayed firm by her sides. Understandable.

"It's ok Mom, you're ok, oh Mom. Ok, ok." I kept repeating it like a mantra. Ok? What was I saying? Mom tore herself from my arms, took two steps back and shattered the night with her tormented scream.

"Ok? Ok? How can it be ok when he hasn't accepted Christ as his personal savior?"

Now it was my turn to take two steps back. My hands in fists, punched down on the air at my sides. Bile started bubbling up from my bowels, fueled by a fiery rage. My fury began to take on words as it flamed upwards, past my solar plexus, my heart, my rising shoulders, my throat.

What kind of cruel sadistic motherfucker do you believe in? Don't you think David has suffered enough? But just before my throat received this, Monica, for the third time, placed her hand gently on my back. What manifested in my mouth was, "I'm so sorry." Mom shuddered and wept as she leaned into my arms. I held her tight and patted and breathed in her sorrow. Over her shoulder, I saw Dad coming down the stairs. His face was locked into a mask. His lips pressed tight into each other forming a straight line, his jaw set hard, eyes looking beyond us and into the horizon. His posture was beaten down by what he had just witnessed, his firstborn son lying there, ravaged by fate. When he reached us, I could see he was too fragile for a hug. It would break him.

"Thanks for calling us Jane."

"I'm sorry Mom and Dad, so very sorry." My voice cracking and horse as I backed away towards the car. Monica was already in the driver's seat. She started the car. My battered car that had gone up and down the rocky driveway, to town, around the island for seven years.

I imagined my folks driving home. Going north towards Kailua town, they would be on Sunset Drive in ten minutes. Would they be able to sleep? Would they hold each other, one keeping the other from breaking into shards? Would they pray for David that he might be spared?

I sat in the passenger seat like a rag doll, checked for my witness star in the southeast. It was there watching passively. I was fully in my body, limp with fatigue and the heaviness of unfathomable grief. I interlaced my fingers and squeezed tight. Then unlaced them and floated my hands to my face, rested my left hand on my cheek. My right hand explored the side of my temple where the impact had killed my brother. I put my palm on my right cheek where the craggy lava had torn into his face. His artist's hands jerked from the handlebars, his right arm, his ribs, hips, sinuous legs ruined. His entire right side had been punctured and clawed by the lava. But his head, his wildly creative and troubled head, took the death knell.

We went down Hospital Road, quiet, made a left onto the Mamalahoa. In Hawaii everyone uses Mauka and Makai. Mauka is the upper side of the mountain, Makai the lower. It's best for directions since Hawaii is made up of mountains, big mountains. The ancient jacaranda tree on the Mauka side, a landmark. Seems it's always covered with clouds of lavender flowers. We continued south past Sam's store. Sam Shumiso has been long dead but it's still Sam's. It clings to the Makai side. We wound south. Still quiet. There was nothing to say. Past Jay Jay's Lau Laus. They make the best on the island. On the weekends they sell Huli Huli chicken from the makeshift grills in the parking lot. We passed Honaunau School where Lea went, Higashi store where Mr. Higashi gave everyone credit. Then right on City of Refuge Road. If you stay on it you get to Honaunau Bay, the Halau for Keoua Canoe Club. But we didn't, we turned right on Painted Church Road. Past the big Norfolk pine covered with bougainvillea, red as blood. On the Mauka side is Painted Church. You can't see it from there, but you can see the plumeria trees sticking out of the lava, generously covered with white, pink and yellow plumerias, graveyard flowers. Then past the immense avocado tree on the bottom of Mrs. Belding's property. Avocados as big as footballs. The dogs eat the ones that drop on the road. Then the mango farm with its ohia post fence. Not nearly sufficient to keep the local kids from stealing mangoes. Let them have the fruit. Their people were here long before we haoles showed up. If you stay on the farm road, it goes all the way to the top of the property, lined by a row of twelve lychee trees. They are tall, wild and unkept. I paid the local kids to climb them, pull off the heavy-laden branches and let them drop to the ground. Lychees have a tough, red bumpy shell so they don't get damaged. They bring good money when they're in season, summer, same as mangoes. We turned right, crunching over the gravel to the carport. I was so tired, my heavy body was melting into the seat. I opened my door. It was heavy as a refrigerator door. I was weak. Beaten on the inside.

Trudging to the kitchen door I remembered the star, the sentinel so far away but seeing me as it always had. I never noticed. It took this tragedy for it to reveal itself. Steady, loyal star.

There was no more denial about David's death. It was real. I saw it unfold. The horror, the shock, the car that kept going up the hill. Acceptance rendered me spent, bleeding tears. Arms like anvils, I staggered to the bedroom, surrendered on my right side to the bed and pillow, still with my sweatpants and T-shirt on. My bed was quicksand pulling my heavy body and head into itself. Sleep immediately began to engulf me.

CRACK!! The jagged edge of a lava rock pierced my skull above my ear and just behind my hairline. A lightning bolt of pain seared into my head, neck, and body. My scream summoned Monica from the couch and into the bedroom. Backlit by the hall light her short curly hair was a halo.

"Oh honey, Janie are you all right?"

No answer.

"Sweet girl, what a terrible thing. Devastating. So hard." She had lost her brother four years before to AIDS. Her handsome brother, blond like her. Athletic and fit like David. This bond linked us in a deep, lasting friendship. "You need to sleep Janie." She ran her fingertips through my hair from my forehead back.

"I know. I'm so tired. So do you, you're the one getting on the plane tomorrow." She continued running her fingertips on my scalp like I've done to Lea to put her to sleep. She didn't stop as she spoke in soft, feathery words.

"Yes, I just had to come to Honaunau one more time, have coffee on the lanai, look down over the ocean, count my blessings to have your friendship."

I was going to tell her how much I would miss her. Beg her to change her flight. Stay for a few more days or a week. It felt selfish. "God bless you for being here with me. I'm so grateful for you." Monica, my friend, my Angel, my nurse, never stopped running her fingers, lighter and lighter, until sleep took me.

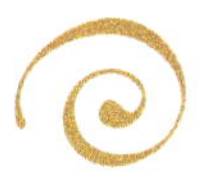

Paul and the Green
Hawaii to Los Angeles
1989

I forgot to say goodbye to Paul. Not so much forgot but refused to concede to his impending death. Lying gaunt and colorless in his hospital bed, he had all the signs of a dying man. Paul had already fought the Hodgkins like a valiant warrior. When the tumor first appeared, he decided it was a swollen gland. He worried but ignored it. I begged him to have it checked out. When the biopsy came back, he trekked to faith healers from Mexico to the Philippines. Bizarre methods were implemented including crystals, chickens, Ayahuaska, and channeling the spirits of saints. The cancer persisted and the tumor grew. By the time he turned to western medicine, the tumor bulged obstinately from the left side of his neck. We had buckets of hope. The battle persisted for over three years. When they quit all the treatments, surgeries, radiation, and chemo, and admitted him to UCLA for the last time, I flew out to LA again.

While I was there, Mom and Dad flew in. At UCLA, the psychiatrist in the cancer wing told Dad it would be good if he could tell Paul he had his permission to die. He suggested that by dying he would let his father down. Mom was incensed that the man would suggest such a thing. Dad couldn't or wouldn't say the words. I've dropped any opinions or judgements about it. Dad did what he could bear. He had already lost one son. He went back to the island the next day. Mom joined him two days later.

"Sis, you've got to get me the hell out of here!" Paul begged. "I'm a lab rat. I don't want to be the Hodgkins poster boy."

"I get it, Paul. Teaching hospital. They won't quit."

"No shit! I'm a human pincushion."

"Ok. John and I will spring you outta here even if we have to kidnap you."

He had already made his case to John, who was with him every step of the way. Not just this leg of the journey but when he flew in from Pahrump for chemo. He stood by Paul's side when he was vomiting from his treatment, drove him around Santa Monica, Venice, Topanga, Malibu, and Westwood, bought the weed and rolled the joints. Pot was good for the nausea, stress, and some laughs.

I was three years sober, living on the Big Island. John called me when they quit the chemo. I knew deep down it was the end of the road. The radiation bombardment had given him leukemia. He had a bone marrow transplant maybe a year before. Everyone was sure this would fix him right up. My sister Lynn was the match. She came out from Indiana, and I flew in from Kona. Before the surgery, a very serious, young Asian doctor marked the exact spot for the extraction. She had me write under the mark in the same black marker, "Usually, one has to at least take me to dinner to see this ass."

It was around Christmas. We went to a party at the Lyons. Samantha was an old friend since Big Sur. Lynn was in a wheelchair and on painkillers. We made the rounds at the party pretending to have a good time and not just whistling in the dark. John hatched a plan with Bruce Langhorn, "Mister Tambourine Man," the guy Dylan was singing about. Bruce had a funky van with a fold-down bed in back. We put a foam on the mattress, covered it with an Indian bedspread, placed cushions against the side and threw pillows around. We three bandits drove to the hospital on a beautiful, early summer morning. Bruce parked in the lot aways from the entrance. We casually strolled to the visitor's desk to pick up our stickers, slapped them on our chests and ambled to the elevators and up to Paul's floor.

"Hey Paul, how's it going, you ready for some green?" Paul had been craving green, hungry for green, trees, grass, hillsides and valleys.

Bruce had a big smile stretched across his face. Seems Bruce always had a smile, a joke, a rhythm, or a song. He was a walking rhythm machine with a djembe, guitar, or of course, a tambourine. He could play any-thing, his head and kinky afro bouncing side to side. If he didn't have an instrument, or two sticks to pound on the table, he would sing. "Talkin' bout hey now, hey now, iko iko all day."

John slipped out of Paul's room to find a nurse. Sweet talked her into loaning him a wheelchair. "My brother needs some fresh air, such a pretty day, am I right?" She knew what he was up to and cried knowing she had seen Paul for the last time. This is the effect he had on people, especially women.

"SCORE!" John announced as he rolled in, popping a wheelie.

"Let's pack your shit and hele on outa here!" John said, slipping into pidgin. To hele is to hurry.

"Hele on!" I said.

Not much packing to speak of, a couple T-shirts, sweatpants, flip flops, a hoodie, toothbrush, razor, and a cassette player with a few cassette tapes. Everything fit into a shopping bag.

"We are outta here," Bruce proclaimed.

"Color me gone! Gone to the green!" Paul bellowed, caught himself and switched to his hospital voice.

"Perfect day for our getaway," I whispered.

We wheeled to the elevator. Bruce backed Paul in, John and me on either side. We weren't alone. A young doctor gave us a weak smile, a couple holding hands acknowledged us with tender nods. We stood shoulder to shoulder sneaking surreptitious glances at each other. Children getting away with something naughty, like blasting off fire-crackers, which is how Bruce, as a kid, lost two thirds of his right index finger. Smirking and giggling, we made it to Bruce's beat-up white van. He could cram an entire band of instruments into it, trap drum set, big juju drum, a couple of djembe drums, guitar, piano keyboard, speakers, console, mike stands, mikes, and yards and yards of electric cords.

"Welcome to your escape van," John exclaimed as he took off his work hat, stretched his arms wide and bowed gallantly. Bruce and John stood on either side and with arms under his head, shoulders, legs and hips, lifted him gently out of the chair and into the van. Gingerly, they placed him on his back. I laid next to him on my right side, slid my right arm under his neck between his shoulders and pillow. My left hand placed on his chest feeling his heartbeat. I nuzzled my face into his cheek.

"I love you my dear brother." We left the lonely wheelchair right there in the middle of the parking lot.

"Love you too sis, love you too," he said in his gravelly voice. His voice was always alto but got deeper from the burns in his throat. He was sleeping in a van near the courthouse, testifying against Manson, when the van caught fire. And he breathed the fumes from burning plastic stored inside. One third of his body sustained second to third degree burns. He was lucky to survive.

Paul made little grunts as we hit bumps and potholes on the way. My cradling him didn't help at all. I tried to comfort him with sounds one would make to soothe a baby, aww, ooh, mmm. We turned west on Wilshire. This would be a long trip, not the restful, languid drive I had imagined. From the shotgun seat, John craned his head around.

"How you doing back there bro?"

Paul, gazing up out the windows, didn't respond.

"We're doing ok. Go slow, careful," I answered, trying to ease the anxiety out of my voice. We made it to Ocean Avenue, a left, then right on the California incline. Tensing my body to stop the little jolts wouldn't help. I let myself sink into the mattress. Paul relaxed a bit too. He was off the morphine drip, which our dear friend Leone, a nurse, would hook up to his port catheter as soon as we got to the Mulholland house. Rented by an army of loving friends, Mulholland house would house his wife Martha and the girls for the duration. They moved from the desert when Paul was admitted to UCLA.

"I gotta stop, gotta get something to drink," Paul announced in a weary voice.

"We have bottled water right here in the van," I countered, removing my arm, which had fallen asleep. Pins and needles assaulted my nervous system.

"Nope, lemonade with ice and a straw, that's what I want."

"Your wish is my command," bellowed Bruce. He drove a few more minutes to a little cafe on the right at the foot of Kanan Dume Road, parked and bounded out. I sat up, smoothed the sweat off Paul's forehead and marveled at the love oozing from my heart. Tears threatened as I saw him as my cute, pudgy little brother, just a year old. Me as an adoring four-year-old, arms around his chest, struggling to carry him. He was a happy baby, my baby brother. I shifted from my reverie just as Bruce ambled out holding the lemonade above his head like a trophy.

"You need help sitting up, Paul?" I asked.

"Yeah, maybe sis."

He was light, hollow feeling as I lifted his shoulders. Bruce handed John the plastic glass, opened the side door, grabbed two big couch pillows from the floor and placed them between Paul's back and the driver's seat.

"That's ok you guys, let me put my legs down while I drink this." Wincing, he let me guide his knees to the edge of the bed. My head was full of worry about the morphine wearing off. We still had the eight-mile drive to Leo Carrillo, then up Mulholland, which would be the worst torture. The precious cup was passed from John, to me, to Paul. He held it in both hands, lifted his head and beamed his grateful smile. Drinking it was a ritual, tenderly witnessed by the three of us. Every moment, every heartbeat would never come again. After he finished a third of it, he handed it to me.

"OK let's hit the road team." The weariness had emptied from his voice.

"I'll hold onto this 'til you are ready for more," I said taking the elixir.

"You finish it sis, I'm done."

"You sure Paul?"

"Yep."

He turned on his right side and coiled his body into a fetal position to sleep. I sat on the bed behind Bruce, sacrament in hand, sipped.

"You guys want some of this? Tastes homemade."

John reached for it. He sipped it like the grape juice in the little glass vials at communion. We went to the Methodist Church every Sunday when we were kids. "This is Christ's blood shed for thee." John handed it to Bruce who also sipped reverently. After it was passed for the second time and finished, Bruce started the van.

The ocean sparkled, the air coming in the back windows, moist and salty, carried the smell of mother ocean. Remarking on the beauty of this day, we reached Leo Carrillo and took a right up Mulholland. Bruce drove slowly and carefully with his cherished cargo. I studied Paul's upper back and belly intently, checking if he was still breathing. Yes, face peaceful, arms tucked together in a sleeper's prayer. The drive was silent, not uncomfortable or pensive silent, only the sound of the engine and gears shifting.

Bruce made a left on a dirt road and there was the modest stucco house, bisque tiled roof, oak slatted hot tub, sycamore and oak trees surrounding it, and a small green grass lawn studded with granite steppingstones to the front door. John got out and opened the sliding doors.

"We're here, Paul, in the middle of the green."

Paul made a muffled sound. "Hmm," he mumbled, raised his head and stretched.

The squealing girls sprinted out of the front door, followed by Martha.

"Daddy, Daddy, Daddy's here!" Claire and Lise tumbled into the van, searching for ways and places to get a good hold, lying their heads on him, squeezing his shoulders, jockeying for positions.

"How's my little Tweezler, my String Bean?"

John, still crouching over Paul, and I sitting by his head, were trapped. Martha stood outside the open door surveying the chaos.

"You girls let him get out first. It's too crowded in there. Welcome to your home away from home Paul."

Martha never called Paul honey, sweetie, darlin' or dear. She had her straightforward way. Paul used up all those terms of endearment. Always had an affectionate title ready. As kids, he called me scrags, my wispy hair usually knotted in a mat at the back my head. It might have been a hurtful tease if not said with fondness. I feigned offense. He never stopped calling me that.

"I made a big pot of beans and rice. Roasted a chicken," Martha announced. "You guys hungry?"

"Sounds so good honey after all the hospital crap." He later had one bite of each.

"Put me on the lawn you guys."

Martha raced to the house for an Indian bedspread. I cleared out. Bruce and John lifted him, same as from the wheelchair, carried him to the lawn and slowly lowered him.

"Ah, the green, great and grand!" Paul remarked in a playful Irish brogue.

The girls surrounded him. Too soon, the pain caught up. His smile faded, replaced by an unavoidable twist on his lips as he pushed them together. Leone stepped forward and kneeled.

"Let's get you inside and hook you up dear."

"Yea, ok, I could use a hookup. C'mon my sherpas."

Through the door, through the living room, incense ineffectively covered the smell of mildew. Down the hall, the main bedroom open and light, was lined with windows and glass doors on two sides, north and west. The bed faced west where massive sycamores and eucalyptus waved on the wind. Out the sliding glass doors on the north side, the ground sloped down the mountain to the faraway soothing sea.

"Perfect." Paul exhaled a huge sigh when laid on the king-sized bed. His port-a-cath was fitted with tubes.

People came to visit from everywhere, bringing food, take-out or homemade, music tapes, musical instruments, pot, flowers and potted plants. Kids played on the south lawn, jumping in and out of the hot tub. Another John, John Anderson began videotaping Paul as he held court with memories, stories and comments.

"Would you just look at all the beauty out there? Amazing!"

Leone brought in a doctor from UCLA who briefly examined, then interviewed him. He told the doctor he thought the cancer was caused by mining boron in Death Valley, breathing the dust. I quietly had another theory. I studied a method of deep tissue massage which attributed fears and negative emotions to parts of the body. The front of the neck is guilt. Years had passed since he had associated with Manson. Before the killings, before things turned ugly, he had left the family and started the long path of deprogramming. Just after Lise was born, the tumor manifested on the left side of his neck. My theory holds that the guilt of not being able to stop the grizzly murders, especially Sharon Tate's, gnawed on him for years, despite his dogged efforts at deprograming. Paul Crockett, an old miner worked with him in the desert. Implementing the philosophy and methods of the Russian mystic George Gurdjieff, Crocket made serious progress in untangling the hold Manson had laid on Paul's psyche. Yet guilt lies deep.

Paul was the one who came up with the motive and notified the Inyo County sheriff's office. He was the main witness for the prosecution. He was the one who toured with Bugliosi and Peter Lawford lecturing on the topic of mind control on the consciousness of American youth. But being lured in by Manson, being in the "family" ate him up from the inside. That was and is my opinion on the matter. He succumbed to the noose of guilt.

Paul had cassette tapes of Irish music, flutes, and songs from the Emerald Isle. Our ancestors. Paul got quieter and went inward as the days passed. Out of the quiet, he would sit up and ask for someone to bring him his tam o'shanter.

"It's on the peg near the door."

"What Paul?" I asked, sure I had heard him wrong.

"My tam o'shanter, there by the door."

"What's a tam o'shanter Paul?"

He wearily laid back down, closed his eyes, and went to sleep. Turns out a tam o'shanter is a traditional Scottish cap menfolk wear. The name derives from Tam O'Shanter, the famed hero of the 1790 Robert Burns poem. He started mumbling in his sleep with a heavy brogue, either nonsensical or Gaelic. Who would know? No one dared change the cassette, it was the sound of the house, comforting and sad. In a lucid moment while I massaged his feet, his skeletal limbs and head, he asked, "think this is it Sis? Am I on my way out?"

"That would be up to God, my dear bro. Am I going too deep?"

"No, it helps."

Martha came in from time to time, bringing tea, coffee, soup, or water. It all went untouched but the water. Sitting on the edge of the bed, she reached under the heel of his foot and raised up his leg.

"Paul, look, you are dying. you aren't going to get better. It's time to say goodbye to the girls." Matter of fact, straightforward Martha. She loved Paul fiercely.

She stopped drinking when Paul accepted that he was an alcoholic and conceded she was too. They built up a community of recovering alcoholics and addicts in Pahrump, organized meetings, held fundraisers for the chamber of commerce, and cheerled Paul when he was the mayor of Pahrump. She was on his team, overlooking his wandering eye, not that they didn't fight about it. Paul was a people-person, she was a Paul-and-the girls person.

The girls spent most of the day in their bathing suits splashing in the lukewarm hot tub, squirting the garden hose at each other, squealing, running, playing make-believe.

Paul had started in on the Cheyne-Stokes breathing, morbidly referred to as the death rattle. The girls didn't come into the bedroom anymore. The horrifying sound is scary for grown folks, let alone little ones. I was familiar with it as my dear friend Susan Branaman began that breathing pattern in her last days. It was in New York City in 1977, I massaged her gaunt body, hoping to ease the awful pain, physical and emotional. There would be more times like these.

I sat in the hot tub with Claire and Lise playing mermaids, making up mermaid songs and counting how long we could stay under water. Suzette came out and leaned over the tub by my head.

"It's close, you should come now."

"Ok Suze, thanks babe," I said, knowing if I went inside, I would witness his last breath. I envisioned

Martha on one side and brother John on the other, holding his hand. I knew, I felt him going. If I went in, the girls would be left alone in the tub, so I stayed, fulfilled my role as queen of the mermaids with my two princesses. It wasn't long before Suzette came out again.

"It's over."

"I know. Would you bring some towels from the line?"

California coastal marine layer drifted in.

"Suze, could you also dry off the girls and help them into their pajamas?"

"We don't want to get out! We want to stay Auntie!"

"It's time to get out. It's getting cold."

I dried off and got into my jeans and T-shirt. In the bedroom, people were filtering out. Leone carefully removed the catheter from the port on his chest, then the urinary catheter and quietly left the room. As I stood in the doorway, John, still sitting at the foot of the bed, looked up in defeat. Like a man come from a battle. I tilted my head and moved in for a hug. Strangely, we didn't sob, or even cry. We hugged tight, then tighter, inhaled together and let go.

We had a ceremony to perform. I leaned down and whispered in his left ear. You are dead now Paul, then massaged a small circle on the top of his head, where the fontanelle would be, then on the tip of his left toe. After the ancient ritual said to release the spirit, we undressed his body, green T-shirt and grey sweatpants. Each with a bowl of water, scented with lavender, we began to wash the body. His face, skin stretched on his wide cheeks and square jaw, his neck. From the left side, John paid special attention to the place the tumor had been. Rinsing and wringing our wash rags, we smoothed across his chest and down his arms, again, special attention to the port next to his heart. In the same moment we reached his hands, wildly creative—mining, polishing stones, welding silver, jewelry-making, flute playing, storytelling, face-holding, child-cradling hands. One finger at a time, the back, the palm, the wrist, then the legs. John washed his genitals. I went slower 'til he caught up. Now shrunken, Paul had such muscular thighs and calves. His body, once compact and strong, lay arid. My mind continued the mantra, *God is one*, breathing long, slow, soft and quiet breaths. His wide feet, the Hawaiians would call "luau feet" were getting cold. John signaled with his eyes that it was time to roll him on his left side. When we turned him, a dark, red stream leaked from the side of his mouth. Mantra stopped. My breath suddenly sucked to the back of my throat. Breathe calm, I told myself. This is the casing, worn out and useless. Paul is not here. He is free to spread his wings into the infinite. Calm again, I rinsed out my rag. John joined me on the right side and began in the middle of his back with long reverent strokes. I went to the back of his head, down the neck, shoulders, and spine. We rolled his rigid body onto his back. To dress him, white was the color, white T-shirt, white drawstring pants. His arms laid at his sides. I rinsed and wrung out the rags, took the two bowls off the bed to the nightstand, then lit a candle. Sitting on the floor facing Paul's body, I placed the candle between me and the foot of the bed. John sat by my side. As I peered into the flame, my body settled. God is watching us, the great mystery surrounded us in silence. The candle flame fluttered like the cosmic dance of Shiva—creating, sustaining, destroying, illuminating, and emancipating. All happening then. Our arms floated up to our chests, palms pressing together, thumbs touching our sternums, big generous inhales, then *Om* . . . The sound low, resonant and long, coming from the depth of our bellies. We bowed our heads and leaned toward the flame. My heart pulsed liked the bright candle.

I counted on my finger pads, three fingers on my left hand counted nine, four fingers on my right counted twelve. When I moved my thumb on the three pads of one finger, I moved to the next. When I finished nine on my left, I moved one pad down on my right. The mantra *Toh Ham Kum Rah* was to be repeated 108 times. Chanting soft and low, the mantra mimicked the rhythm of a heartbeat. Leaning forward with each repetition, my body moved as though I was riding a camel across a vast desert. When we reached 108, I rang a small Tibetan bowl John had placed at my right knee. I had been concentrating on the mantra, the counting, and the steady rhythm so deeply that all thoughts had been swept clean from my consciousness. In the quiet eternal moment, the mantra walked on. Our hands floated up for another *Om*, closing the ceremony.

John stood and opened the bedroom door. I sat in silence as Martha and the girls came in. Lise and Claire were holding bouquets of wildflowers in one hand and crayon-colored cards in the other. These were the tasks they carried out while the ceremony was performed. I stayed cross-legged on the floor as they hurled their bodies on Paul's.

"I love you so much Daddy," each girl proclaimed over and over until their voices shattered into sobs. Martha stepped forward and placed her hands on their shoulders.

"Paul, go with all this love around you, take it with you," she said, tears washing her cheeks, dripping from her jaw.

Everyone filtered out except John, Leone, and me. I emptied the bowls on the grass outside the sliding door, took them to the kitchen sink. John moved the flowers and covered Paul's body with a white sheet. Leone picked up the phone from the far nightstand and began making calls. I came in from the kitchen, noticed four vials of morphine on the bedside table, scooped them up with my right hand, and with my left hand began picking up the flowers and placing them on top of the sheet.

"What have you got there, honey?"

"Flowers, just arranging them."

"No, there in your right hand." She spoke in a calm voice as one would speak to a child who was upset.

"Keepsake," I mumbled.

"I can keep them for you Jane," she said, as she steadily moved toward me.

"No. It's ok, I'm ok." Standing in front of me she cupped her hands around my right hand, brought the tight fist close to her face. One finger at a time, she pried each finger from the fist, speaking in the same sweet voice.

"I know it's ok, you're ok. You have been so brave, such a good sister," she said, still prying, one by one. Gripping my hand in her left, she slipped her fingers deeper into my right palm until she reached my index. Wrapping her fingers around the vials she continued. "Look, I'll keep them right here," she said as she dropped the vials into the left pocket of her powder-blue work shirt and patted the pocket with her right hand. "Here, right next to my heart. They're safe. Don't worry." She looked tenderly into my bewildered eyes, gave me a long hug and left the room.

Sunset had finished an hour before. The sky still held faint mauve and blue light. Unable to leave the room, I sat in the armchair next to the bed. Putting both hands on my face, elbows on my knees, leaned into the undertow, heaved and sobbed.

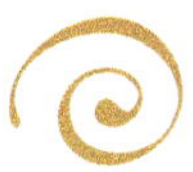

Fear and Loathing in Washington
Santa Monica
2016

The alarm jolted me awake at 5:15 am. It was a mistake. I had set it for 7. Fear, like rising floodwater, oozed under the door. Not unusual lately—terror, worry, and anxiety pulled at my solar plexus like a hysterical child. Thoughts raced. The sound machine, meant to mimic the soothing ocean, was tinny, unconvincing. It did mask the sound of the clock marking four long years, one tick at a time. Einstein once said, "As our circle of knowledge expands, so does the circumference of darkness surrounding it." I must be a genius. This immense darkness threatened to swallow me.

The election brought such a forceful current of dread, I couldn't see his face or hear his name without a wave of nausea. His voice, his gestures, his cruelty and lies, like claws on a blackboard. When hope waned on election night, I went to the den, curled into the fetal position as groans came from the living room. We were doomed. I couldn't go home, I couldn't join in. I clutched my knees and cried.

The next morning, I woke. Was it a night terror leaving a stain on morning? No.

Go outside or hole up? Somnambulating, I went out. The sun was in the sky. Trees stood where they were. A young man on a ladder was painting our building turquoise, my favorite color. A Mayan with a moon-shaped face and dark gentle eyes looked down.

"*Como estas?*" he asked.

"*Tengo mucho miedo,*" I replied.

Knowing his status I said, "You should be afraid too."

He put down his brush and looked directly into my eyes. "Fear is a sickness."

"It's contagious." I softened my shoulders.

"Hope, *esperanza* is also contagious."

"Why not choose hope?"

In the following days, out of desperation, I ramped up my meditation, yoga, bike rides, and AA meetings. I knew I wouldn't drink but daily anguish made me wish for relief.

I booked a flight to Washington, using the air miles saved for a languid trip to Hawaii. Once there, I joined a sea of pink heads bobbing against the sky. For a few hours, I surrendered to the pulse of global hope and resistance

Our voices surged upwards in rhythmic chants. Kind people smiled and laughed through the looming darkness. Roaring rivers of spontaneous cheers swept through the immense crowd. Courageous, we faced the juggernaut, stormed the Bastille.

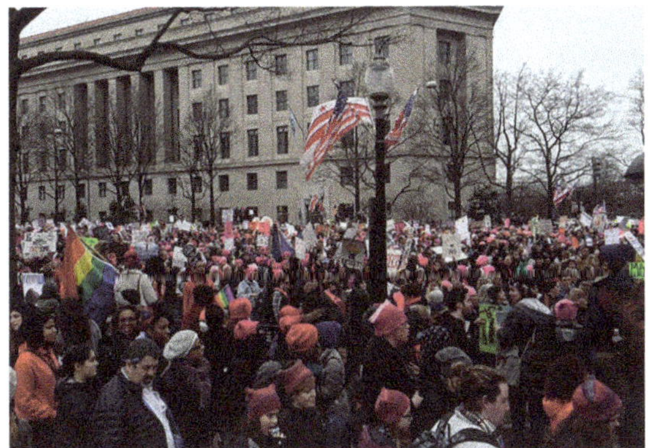

Pink Hats

We raised our fists in defiance, funneling our rage to the horizon. We, who see the precious earth tortured by insatiable greed. We, who watch compassion, truth and liberty wane.

Together, will we slay the dragon? We, who were here before?

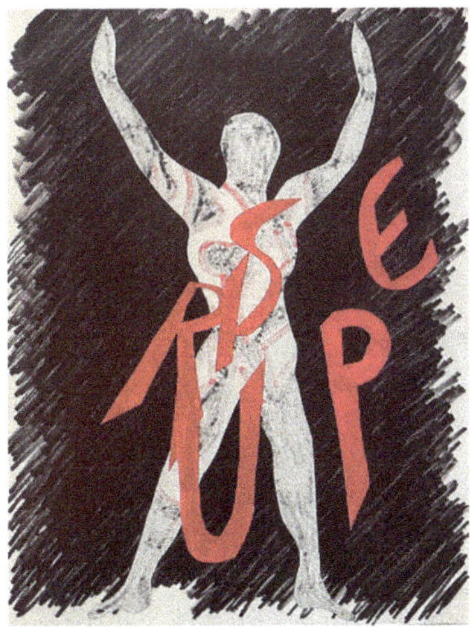

Rise Up

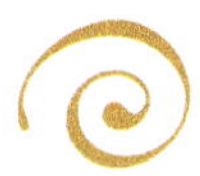

Blustery Beach Walk
Santa Monica
2020

The beach offering that day was the maniac wind. Charging southeast, whipping up clouds of sand that had become weaponized. Little needles pierced every exposed part of my body.

Makes sense the tribes crossing the Sahara wore complete body covering. I wore a baseball cap, wide sunglasses, a long-sleeve rash guard, a neoprene vest, and a windbreaker. The hood of the windbreaker over my cap was tied tightly around my sunglasses and mask. I had on 3/4 length yoga pants and flip flops. My lower calves and feet were protesting.

On the path to the boardwalk, bikers crouched low battling the force. I leaned into it. Few people were out, only a handful.

I arrived at the boardwalk and turned left toward the ocean. I could hear the sand pelting the side of my hood. My ears, thankful to be covered. I turned my face to the left and pushed towards the roiling ocean. I reached the water's edge. Took off my flip flops and put them in the deep pockets of the windbreaker. It was low tide, but the wind ignored that fact and blew the bubbly froth onshore. No blowing sand then, as it was held down by a wide, wet surface. But the wind! I made a right and hurled myself north toward the sea wall. A mile and a half. I knew it would feel like five. Heaving, thinking of turning back, I trudged on.

Lifeguard stands shrouded by whirling sand marked my progress. Eight, six, four, two. Next the numbers jumped to eighteen, seventeen, and fifteen. Don't ask me why. I made it to the sea wall, thanking the long pile of boulders for shielding the wind a bit. I enjoyed it for a while before turning back. With my foot up on one of the rocks, I stretched. One, then the other. I was stalling. Time to go. Turning back, I became a human kite, forgetting that would happen! I'm not a runner; I'm a power walker. But then, I had a wind engine begging to run.

After having my head down so long, I looked to the sky. Clear as a blown glass bowl, betraying the swirling tempest wind. The great dome was sapphire at the top, graduating to azure, and finally celeste on the edges. The sea was avocado green, sparkling with white caps, all the way to the horizon.

Having virtually flown to tower eight, I turned my body toward the boardwalk and readied myself for the onslaught. I turned my face to the right, bearing it. It would be at my back once I reached the path. Sure enough, I was lifted, joyous except for the sand that burrowed into the back of my calves, almost there. First the circular upward climb, then over Pacific Coast Highway, then a long ascent to the park. I was into the wind but relieved of piercing sand. Looking up, a stand of palm trees bowed away from the source. Breathing heavily, I arrived at the bike rack, unlocked my bike, and let the wind blow me home.

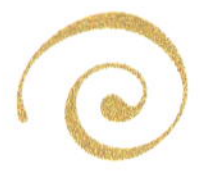

What I Miss About Hawaii
Santa Monica
2023

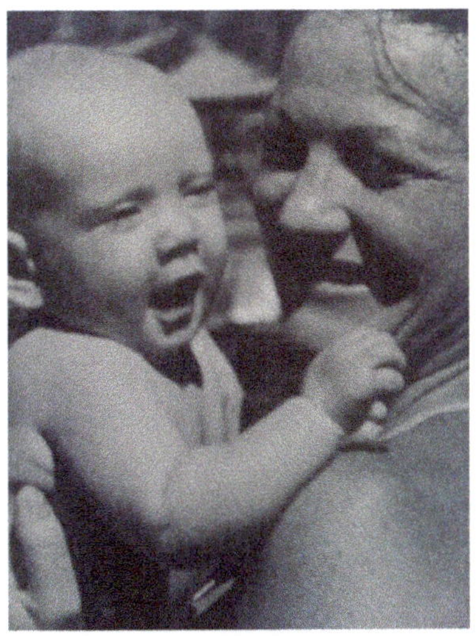

Lea and Me

I miss cradling my little baby in my arms.

I miss being Mom to a little girl who needs me, my attention, my love. Time spent Sundays at Ho'okena Beach with family and friends. Watching the band of little ones playing with sticks, eating sand, running to and from the waves.

I miss the smell of flowering coffee trees, Honaunau, that half-moon cut out from the side of Mauna Loa, Pele's Mountain. This one lush place is chock full of intense beauty. In pidgin it's *choke*. *Choke lei, choke* grinds (food), *choke aloha*.

I miss the sound of banter from a gaggle of locals, punctuated by waves of laughter. I don't miss vog, the acid smell and haze. It's Tu Tu Pele's afterbirth that blocks the sun and its reflection on the sea.

I miss the leeward side, how the vast Pacific stretches west into infinity. Within her, the whales bellow, their

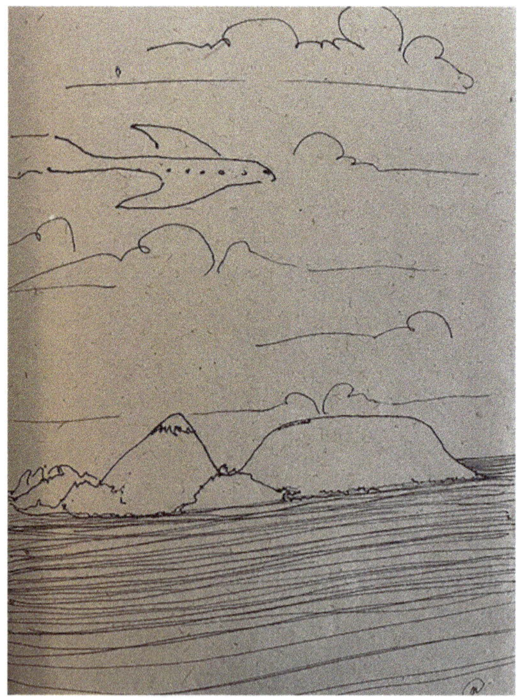

Plane Over Hawaii

songs bouncing off the seamounts halfway around the world.

I miss the humility of knowing there are creatures on our planet with much bigger brains than we puny humans, thinking we're the end all and be all.

And the sky! Blue—lighter close to the horizon, deeper sapphire at the apex. The luminous clouds are so animated they have lively conversations.

I need to go back soon.

I miss the mango farm. Picking mangoes in my overalls. Taking them to market. Sorting the A grade for selling from the B grade (bitten by fruit flies) that get cut up for freezing. Making mango cobbler. We don't have enough freezer space, so we dole them out in the neighborhood.

I miss Hawaiian sunsets and knowing my parents are just up the hill in the big house. Especially my mom, with her welcoming heart who would eagerly take Lea or any of her grandkids at a moment's notice.

I miss swimming with spinner dolphins in Kealakekua Bay, almost a daily ritual, swimming miles when the dolphins were there. If there weren't dolphins, we would crawl along the warm Hawaiian water to Captain Cook's monument. One mile as the crow flies, unless we swam along the side of the bay overlooking the coral.

I miss the moist air, filling out my skin, my eyes. Saltwater waiting just down the hill, all year round. Brilliant sunsets.

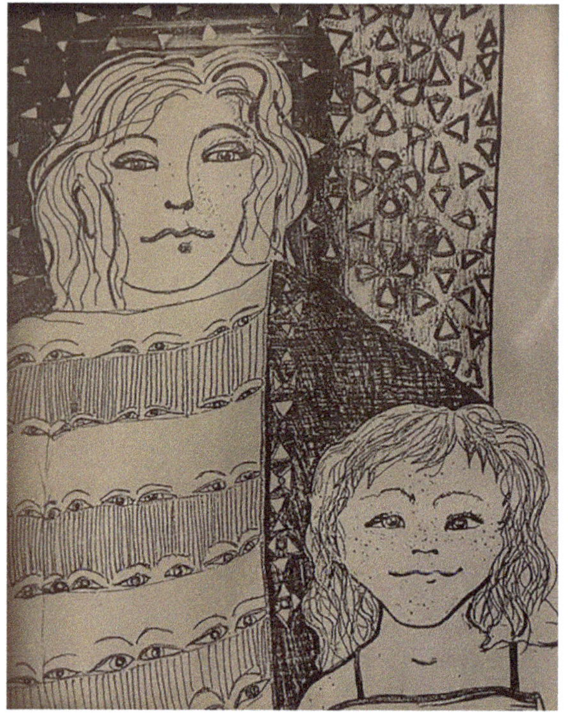

Me and Lea

I miss driving Lea to school past the big jacaranda tree, purple cloud of flowers. The smell of coffee roasting, or flowering relative of gardenia. The Mamalahoa Highway high above the ocean, flanking the side of Pele's Mountain, Mauna Loa.

I miss making yards and yards of silk batik in the carport, my studio. The smell of hot beeswax sometimes attracting jealous bees. Hanging them, twelve yards at a time. Cutting silk at dusk on the lanai while the neighbors drank beer and talked story, punctuated by gales of

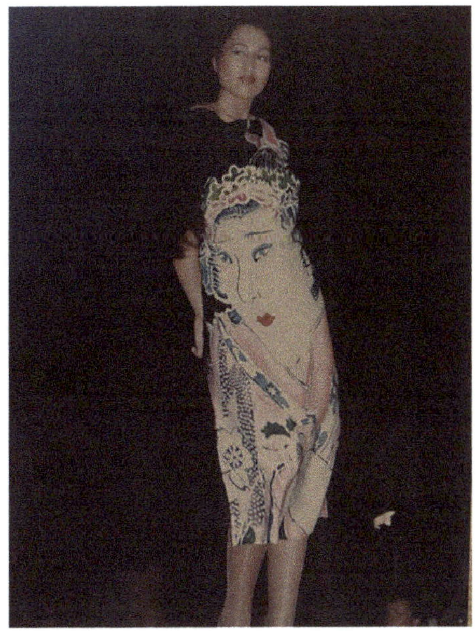

Batik Dress

laughter. Then, fashion show models were my beautiful friends, hula dancers, or women from my canoe club. I paid them all in silk. I miss being interviewed, having the shows covered by *West Hawaii Today*.

I miss winning canoe races, cutting through the waves. Feeling fearless and brave. Paddling 40 miles with my crew from Molokai to Oahu. Sitting in seat one, calling the changes. Being in a Master's crew that couldn't be beat for a whole season. Pictures in the sporting section of the paper.

I miss being in my thirties, sleek and tan. Smooth face devoid of wrinkles except for a few laugh lines.

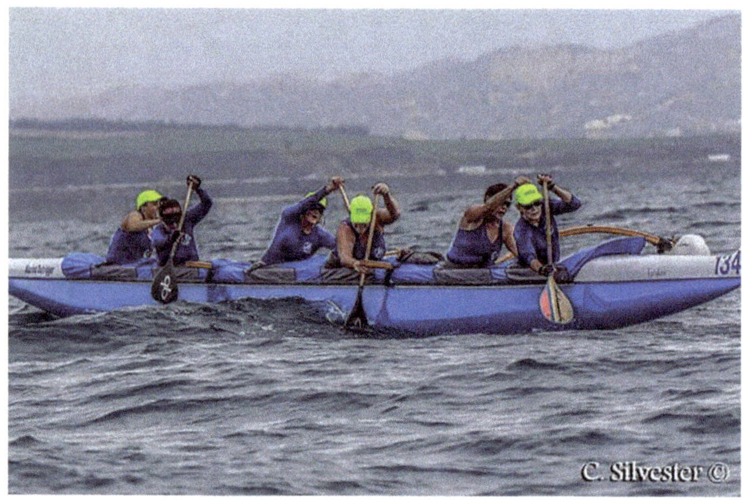

Outrigger Paddling

Wearing flip flops all day, every day. Living on Painted Church Road. Listening to the kids chatter and squeal as cars ran over the avocados they put there, and *chout ca comine*, cracking macadamia nuts with a hammer.

I miss driving to Hilo south way through Volcano, passing South Point, through Naalehu, Mauna Loa on the left, vast ocean on the right.

I miss rolling green hills, Ohia trees standing in lava fields. Picking the red Lehua Flowers, like bursting fireworks. Making Haku head leis for each woman in my crew.

I miss opening in a gallery. Being quasi-famous. Speaking pidgin, joking with the locals. Having a house, a lanai, an expansive view of the Pacific. Being a Big Island Girl.

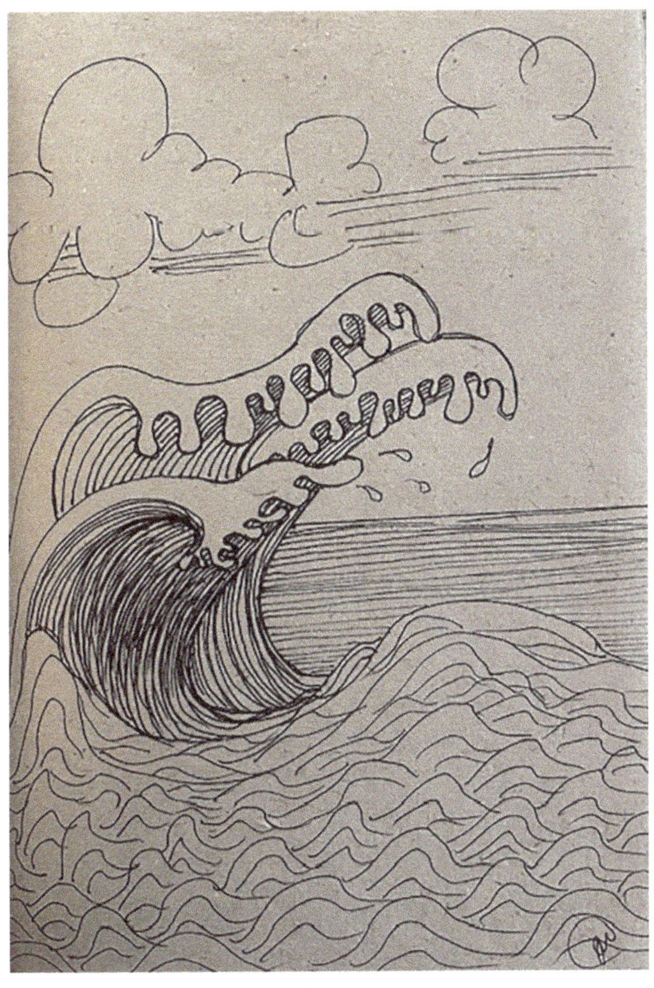

Wave

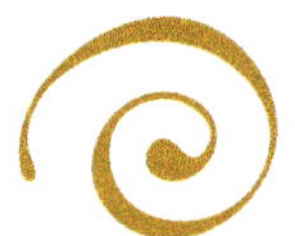

Poems

Dearly Departed

Infinite Light

Hawaii

Final Reflections

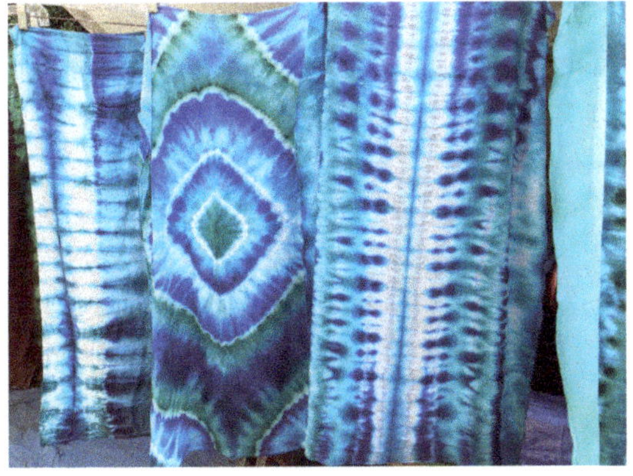

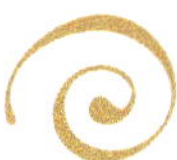

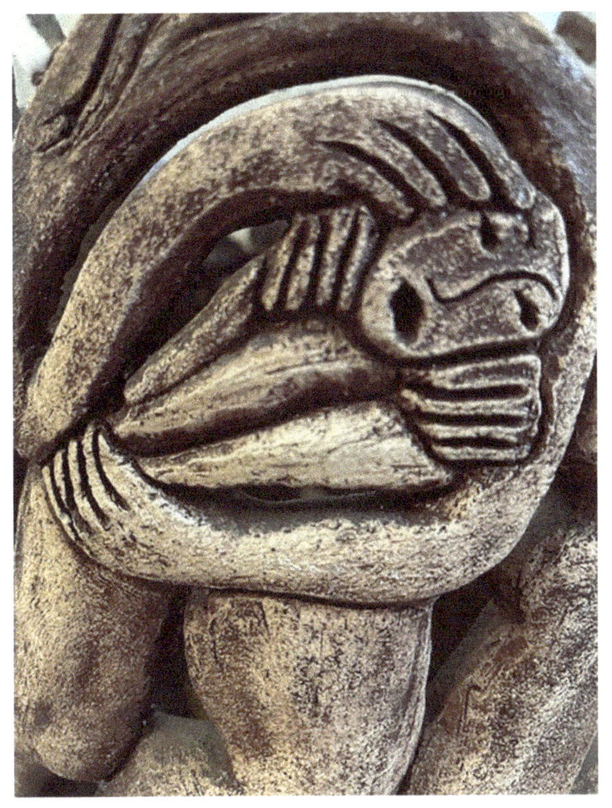

Dearly Departed

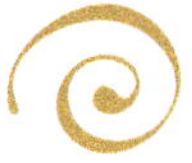

Cry Mama

For Mom

Two of your boys are dead and gone.
Twenty-nine years doesn't seem so long.

Cry Mama cry.

All of your babies have babies,
who also have babies, who will never know you.

Cry Mama cry.

Heavy hard memories in my head,
I'd rather have a song or a poem instead.

Tell me now Mama, what will we do,
without your cackling laugh, and your pat-pat too?

Rock your baby and cry Mama cry.

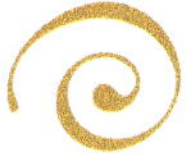

Debutante

For Suzette Elliot

The debutante's on food stamps,
she has taken to her bed,
with between a forty and eighty
percent chance of being dead.

They've taken out her kidney,
but can't cut the tumor out.
It's on the big nerve superhighway,
the doctor has no doubt.

Thank God, she quit smoking
and she doesn't have a cough.
When she called me up to tell me,
we laughed our asses off.

I love my cowgirl debutante
with all my heart and breath.
I love her through this nightmare,
I just love her to death.

Joyce

For Joyce Kasky—gypsy gal, friend in Big Sur

Was it you I saw running naked in the rain?
Weren't you just on your death bed leaving,
with your face to the sky and your arms spread wide?

Was it you just now I was seeing,
with your hourglass figure, your hair tumbling down,
gypsy bangles on your ankles and your arms?

Was it you set free in the spring rain falling?
Was it you dear friend—or was it me?

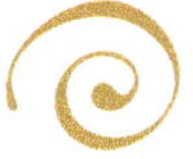

King of Cool

For the remarkable Bob Branaman—artist, beatnik,
part of the Kerouac / Ginsberg beat scene

A swath of jagged mountains makes
from fallen geometric shapes,
faces every type and size,
gaze into each other's eyes.

City nudes lounge and romance,
while those in redwoods writhe in dance.

Honest portraits see your soul,
elaborate lizards play the fole.
Circles curl up in the sky,
and opening, make angels cry.

Authentic Beatniks go extinct,
Ferlinghetti's pen runs out of ink.
Rinpoche revealed the jewel,
that day we lost the King of Cool.

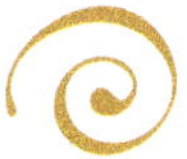

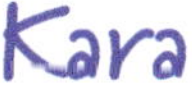

Kara

In memory of Kara, infant daughter of my dear friends,
Lily and Dave Dulan

Before
your words
could be
spoken,
before
your heart
could be
broken,
before
the uprising
sun,
you were
gone.

Before
your parents
both waited,
sacrificed,
anticipated,
a girl,

wished for
so long
you were
gone.

Before
the heavens
could open,
before
the angels
were hoping,
before rain,
before pain,
or the sun,
you were
gone.

Tuesday night,
bright angels
surround you
in your sleep,
sought out
and found
you
to liberate,
greet,
and unbound
you
from this world.

You stayed
for such a
brief measure
little sister,
to give us
the treasure
of knowing
when all's
said and done,
we are
one.

This truth,
this light,
still binds
us,
surrounds us
in our hearts,
finds us
in the love
that is second
to none.

We are one,
we are one,
we are one.

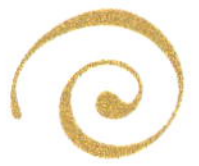

Linda's Leaving

For Linda Cross, my best friend in Big Sur and Chile

As sunset to our
sweetheart comes,
as gentle friends
surrender her
to light, still brighter
than the sun,
with lovers still
defending her.

We struggle with
the shadow past,
our tendency
to hold on fast.
Good God will
have her way, at last.

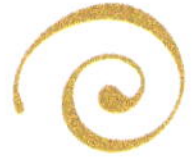

Mr. Tambourine Man

*For Bruce Langhorn (Tambourine Man) who played the
tambourine in Bob Dylan's band*

Mr. Tambourine Man has taken to his bed,
hospital rails to keep him in,
he won't leave 'til he's dead.
His voice still has the low buzz,
his lips that wicked smile.
Me and Honey came today
to sit with him awhile.

Honey brought a tiny banjo,
A gift from Joan Baez,
a hollow silver locket
with a note inside that says,
He's such a great musician,
his ear and sound so fine.
We will meet up down the road
when we catch that number nine.

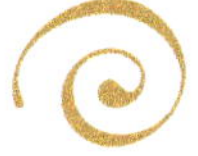

Six Stanzas for Steve

For Steve Stroud, my dear friend from Big Sur, Chile, and New York

That lopsided smile,
lumbering gait,
fierce, gentle heart,
refusing to wait.

Bathed in abundance,
meeting your king
on equal footing,
said the *I Ching*.

Valkyries of Valhalla
carried you home.
Now, safe in the emptiness,
never alone.

Calm, powerful presence
on Odin you stand.
A gesture of peace,
yet sword in hand.

Free now to orbit
the invisible sun,
infinitely circling,
all is one.

The *I Ching* said also,
be joyful, don't cry,
we're always together
you and I.

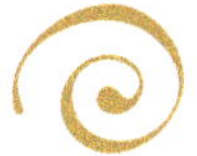

The Guide

For Shiley Palmer, my AA sponsor

Your smile is a sunrise
pulsating light,
opening the door
of forgiveness.

Your voice is the trade wind,
gentle and warm,
speaking the truth
as a witness.

Your uncommon kindness
is guiding me inward,
to my own self,
the place I belong.

And like all epic journeys,
the heroine finds
she's always been,
already home.

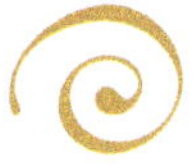

Valkyries

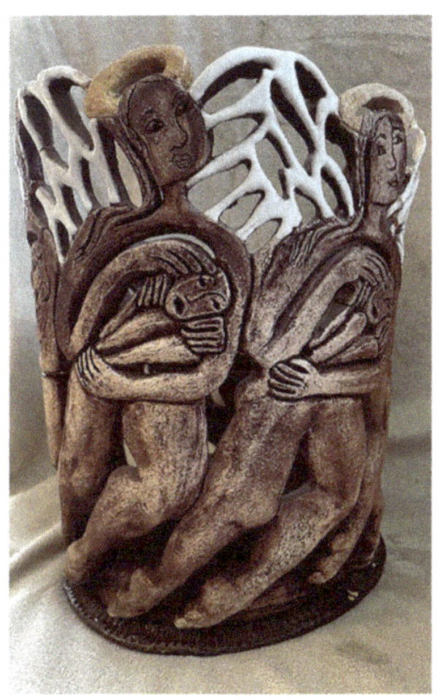

Valkyries

Angels with thighs like pistons
carry the wounded home,
wrapped in a fetal position,
giving up all that they own.

Sinewy thighs, biceps and wings
are up to the task,
lifting the fallen warriors,
hollowed out, shell and mask.

Of one, who was once so certain
of everything she surveyed,
given no choice but an inner voice,
which she seldom heard or obeyed.

She, the muscle-bound angel
over the battlefield soars,
shielding her broken soldier
from chaos and the horrors of war.

Pulsing her wings of thunder
to pummel waiting air,
she sounds the pounding rhythm,
the syllables of her prayer.

She offers no explanation,
no theories of heaven or hell.
Mute in her duty, she surges
to the refuge she knows so well.

Into the eye of the cyclone
with her gentle, powerful force,
back to the place we all come from,
the eternal immutable source.

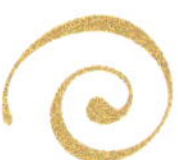

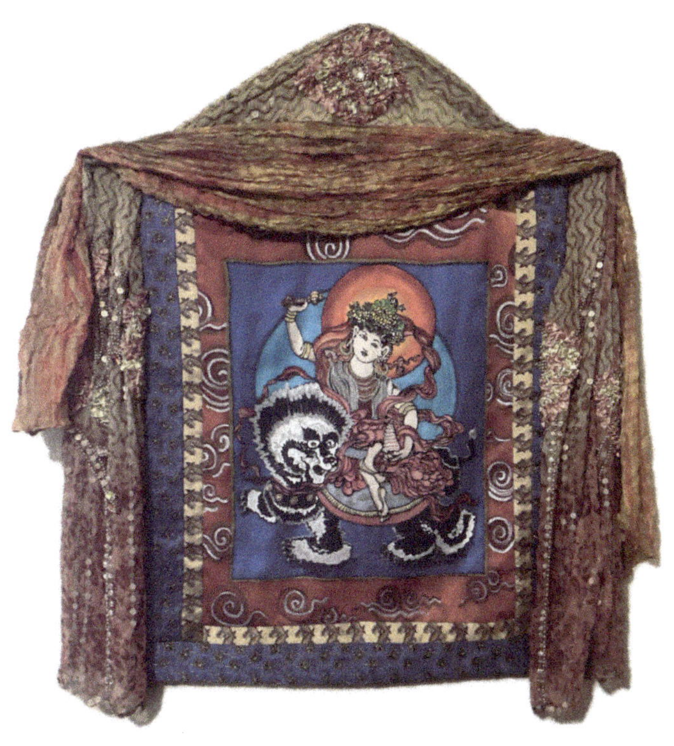

Infinite Light

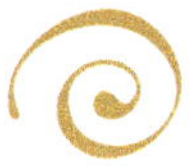

Amnesia

Cradle to grave I forget you,
over and over again.

Angel of peace with silence you speak,
yet your light slips right out of my hand.

Life after life, I have left you.
Blinded by chaos, I fell.

You, consistently offering heaven,
absentmindedly, I chose hell.

Maybe someday, I'll remember so fully,
I won't have to hide behind all the clocks
I'm using to count—how many times I have died.

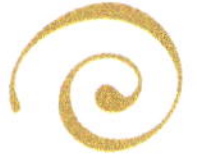

Deathless

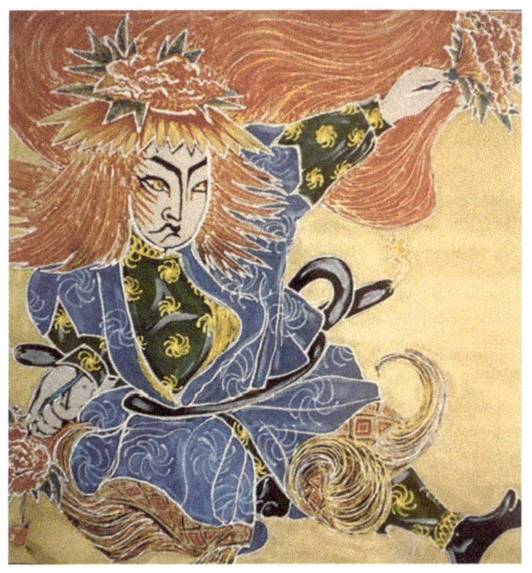

Lion Dancer

Essence to essence, dust to dust,
we all go down the way we must.

Some go swiftly, some go slow,
there is no account for how we go.

Some pacified, accept their fate,
and gracefully capitulate.

Others kick and scream and fight
against the dimming of the light.

So seek that which no change anoints,
no feeble eye, no creaky joints.

And by no hand will ever die,
never being born is why.

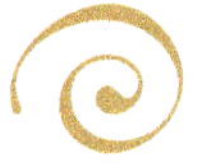

Flightless Bird

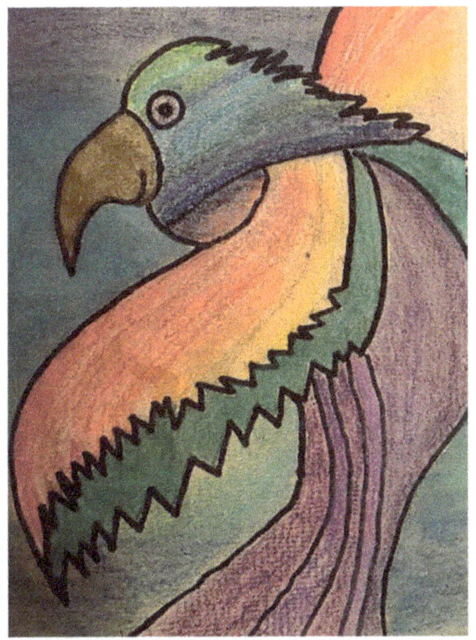

Parrot

That abandoned flightless bird
came again today,
walking on its gnarled claws,
nothing new to say.

—— Jane's World ——

No sight, no sense, no color,
no memories to share,
no dance, no chance to change things,
mutely standing there.

If she wasn't deaf, I'd tell her,
remind her she's not real,
just a phantom conjured,
a wound that will not heal.

Mute teacher has forgotten
the lesson she's about,
beneath her waxy feathers,
a song needs crying out.

For the broken, caged and voiceless,
victims of warfare,
for the battered, choiceless
in terror-shocked despair.

Innocence ignored,
history unheeded,
once we had a garden,
all we ever needed.

Pray for peace, pray for the world,
and for the flightless bird,
that she'll grow wings, find her voice,
and finally be heard.

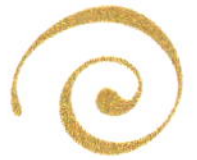

Om Mani Padme Hum

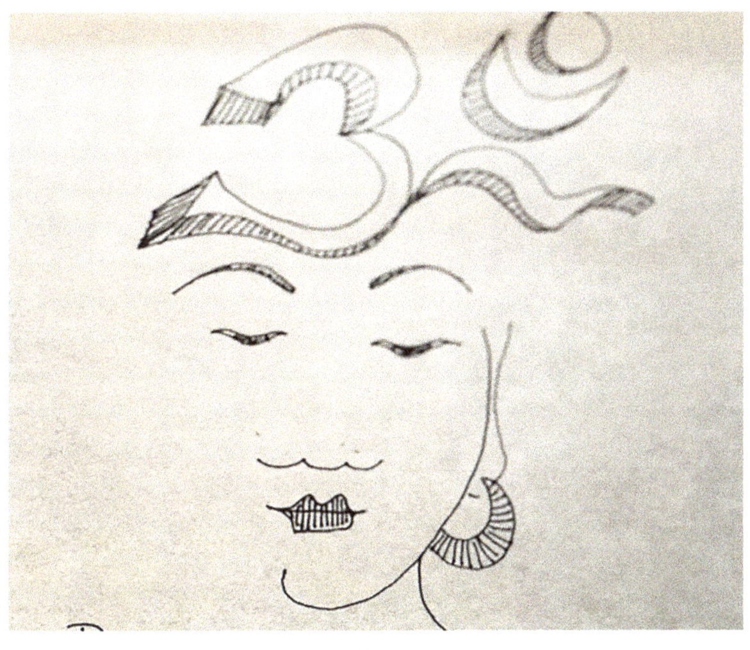

Om

The moon lifts up the climbing tide,
reflects the sun, her loyal guide.
Om mani padme hum

Pipers charge and then retreat
to the sea's hypnotic beat.
Om mani padme hum

Clouds unfold across the sky,
seagulls pattern soaring by.
Om mani padme hum

Swirling clouds with wind and rain,
cleanse the tableau once again.
Om mani padme hum

Dharma wheel turns round and round,
grinds the past into the ground.
Om mani padme hum

Mountains pierce the ceiling,
then crumble into dust again.
Life sustaining mother earth,
still indifferent to their birth.
Om mani padme hum

Born to die and born again,
impermanence will always win.
Om mani padme hum

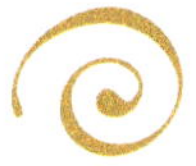

Seeing My Teacher

The mystic maestro,
the harlequin king,
the brother, the bearer
of the invisible ring.

The sure-footed sherpa,
the man in the wall,
the Buddha at Nara
that's forty feet tall.

The wild-eyed gypsy,
dancing, dripping in sweat,
the high-flying condor
lifting over regret.

The messenger diplomat,
lunatic, shrink
to a teetering world,
balanced close to the brink.

The clown on a tightrope
holding an egg,

the houseboy who stands
so long on one leg.

The light in the tunnel
holding fast through the years,
a torrent of laughter,
an ocean of tears.

The mandarin emperor,
blue and gold in brocade,
with a long thin mustache
on a carved throne of jade.

The shapeshifting shadow,
emerald pillar of light,
a boy with a secret
holding a kite.

Alfa Omega,
are you, my king?
Or a carnival ride,
where I missed the brass ring?

Now that I know
I can leave with free will,
my brother, my friend,
are you seeing me still?

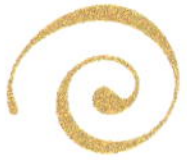

The Crone

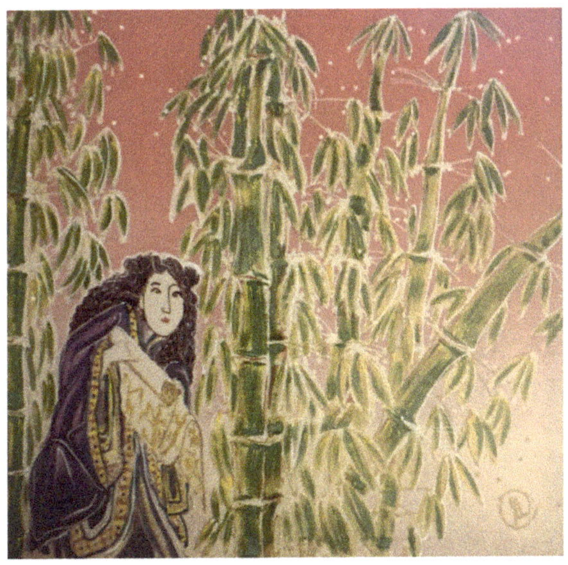

The Crone

She is a laughing, loving, leading lady,
who may trick you to thinking you're going half crazy.
She's the joker and maker of the Dervishes dance,
the dark Goddess Kali, with sword and lance.

She came the first day dressed as a spider,
to spin the world with the stuff inside her.
She called for the wind, cried for the rain,
invented sound reason, centered and sane.

She gathered her children on the tortoise's back,
keeping them safe from disease and attack.
She gave them choice and set them free,
to live in peace and liberty.

She's the hand of mercy that cradles your face,
the shaman's sacred healing place.
Feel her breath on your skin, the soul of laughter,
and heart of fun, apologizing to no one.

Her mind extends to the whitening sky,
thoughts like blackbirds flying by.
The memory mother and daughter of pain,
birthing herself, again and again.

She's a fierce protector of the battered and hurt,
head in the sky, bare feet in the dirt.
Know her like the river knows the riverbanks,
honor her daily in humble thanks.

She's the mystery song forever sung,
just as sure as the stars in the heavens are hung.
She's the dark blessed womb we all come from,
and will welcome us home when the dance is done.

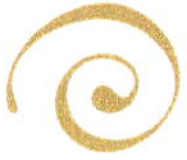

Tigers

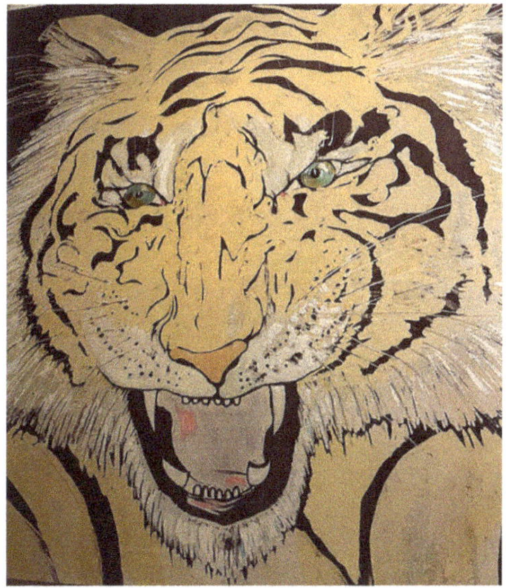

Tiger Face

Tigers crouch in silence on the edge of reason, ready to pounce your fragile form. They have been waiting longer than death in the ancient snow of consciousness, perfect hunters—you are prey, in the way you so fear them.

Impossible fear sees no beauty. If you run, you fall. If you fall, you dissolve, and become the jungle floor. Through hollow eyes, flows the river. From your mouth, spotted orchids grow, taste of vanilla fills the palate. Rain forest weeps, veiny spider creeps along the glass threads of her diamond-studded web.

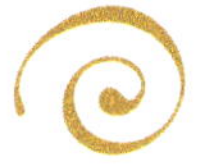

While You Were Sleeping

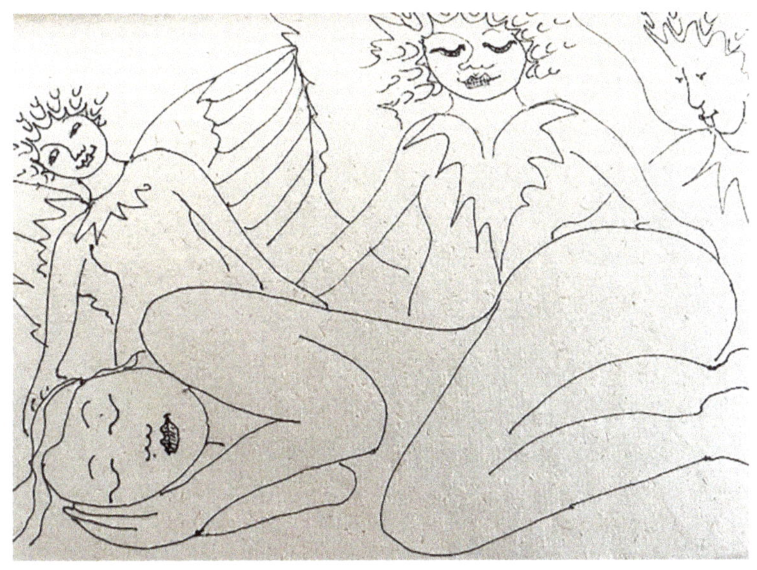

While You Were Sleeping

While you were sleeping,
the angels came down
to watch you more closely,
and hover around.
Crouched carefully by you,

they cradled your cheek,
smoothed out your hair,
held onto your feet.
In cascading showers
of tenderness deep,
gave you love that would fill you,
no loneliness keep.

While you were sleeping,
you were honored and blessed,
sung to and clung to,
embraced and caressed.
You were soothed and made holy,
embodied in light,
'til you beamed like a candle
there in the night.

While you were sleeping,
this world drifted by,
great cultures were birthed
only later to die.
Eons gave forth
in the blink of an eye.

While you were sleeping,
love reigned for your sake,
great rivers of love,
more than you could take.
More than you could dream of,
if you were awake.

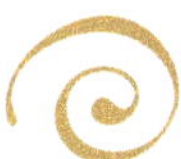

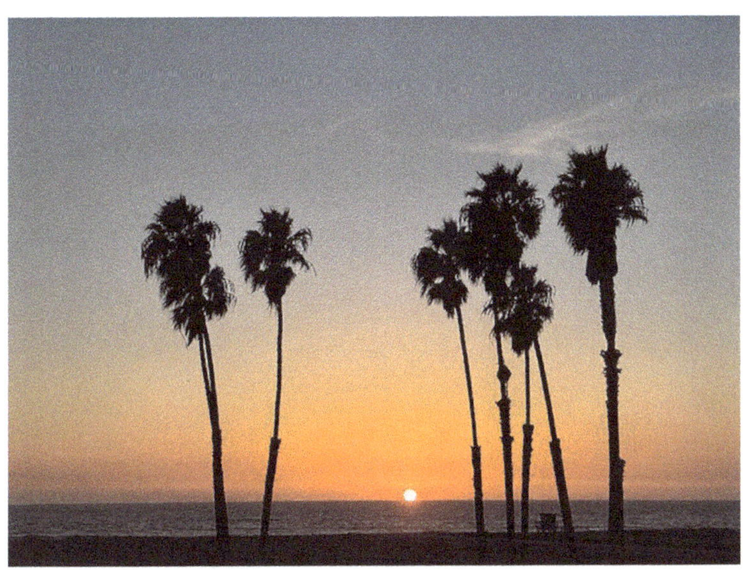

Hawaii—The Big Island

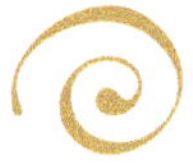

Big Island Song

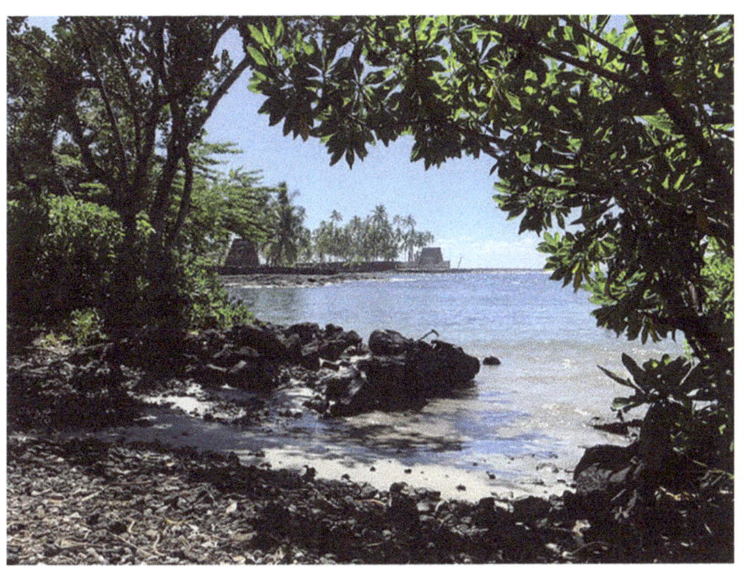

Honaunau

Big Island Song
rushes on like a waterfall,
with willingness, wonder of all.
Too big to sleep, you fill my eyes
with highest skies,
pierced by Mauna Kea's snowy spire.

Jane's World

You are the mother of
nature's garish rush on the world,
sunsets gash of mango light,
orchids inner sex unfurled.
You are the soft coo of bashful doves,
the starting place of rich and salty loves.
You are the pidgin-speaking barefoot boy,
who plays in the road of simple joy.

My home wrapped on all sides in royal blue,
you spend your days giving diamonds to the sun.

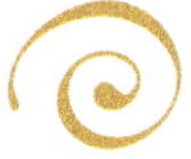

Colors

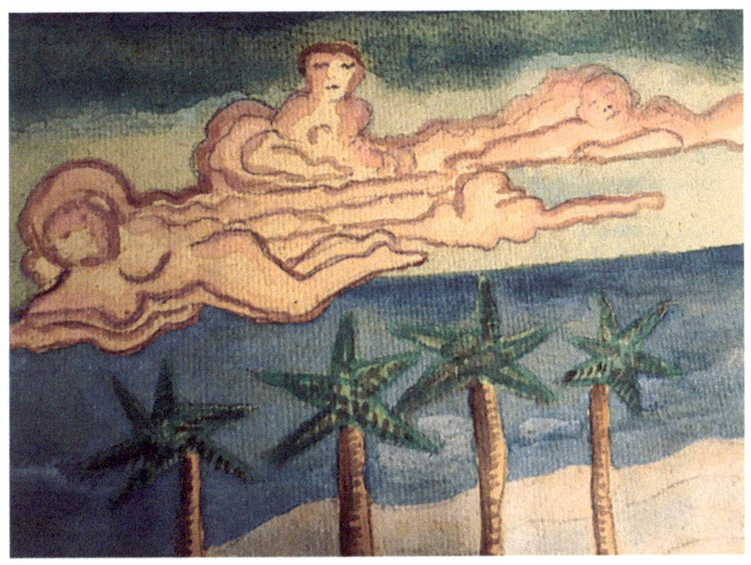

Lazy Lady Clouds

There's no more brilliant blue than the sky at Punalu'u,
spread on Mauna Loa, Pele's breast.

And I've surely never seen a more satisfying green,
than the wild Waimea pastures laid at rest.

Jane's World

The red of passions flood, as the Goddess Pele's blood
spills from earth's core to high lehua flower.

All the gold on Kona side, on the leeward sea spreads
wide when the sun is taking refuge in the west.

More majestic than a crown, as the sun is going down
and shimmers on the far horizon crest.

It seems Big Island's colors shine brighter than all others,
here in the velvet of sweet tropic air.

My hand will choose these hues like returning to a lover,
being never better loved than being there.

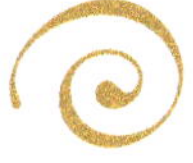

Deep Water Woman

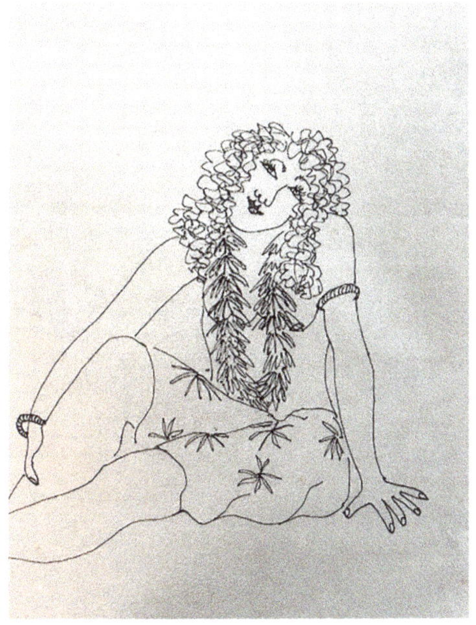

Deep Water Woman

Deep water woman crawls along the healing sea,
hair expanding into forever,
webbed feet and fingers pull and push through time,
through a lacy veil of silver fish,

a diamond pattern from sun on the water,
that falls upon the sandy bottom,
upon the pink blush of dolphin flanks,
upon the vast sea unseen,
reaching around the world as far as the whale song,
as deep as the heart can be.

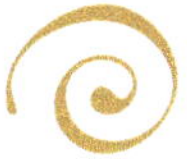

Honaunau (place of refuge)

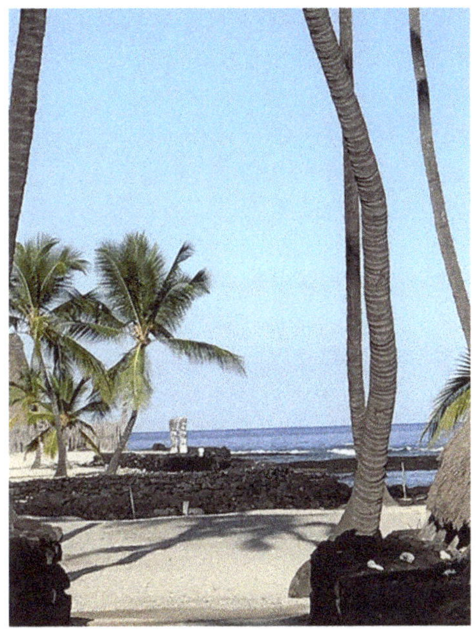

Pu'uhonua

Three a.m. in Honaunau, sleep refuses me.
The full moon makes her tapa patterns
on the window screen,
the velvet wind knocks together banana leaves.

———— Jane's World ————

This is the place of refuge, Pu'uhonua,
where ancients swam or ran from certain death
to the safety of Kahuna Hale.

This place holds my heart.
It's violent colors, deep water
where no dolphins, but whales came today.

The place of hurt and healing,
where memories wash like tropical rain.

Roosters crack the silence,
air heavy from Mauna Loa summit
comes down to my bedroom,
a dog barks.

Icy wind rolls down the mountain
effortlessly surrendered to gravity.

Imagine dark night, one mile deep,
the mouth of Kealakekua Bay,
the giant, silent sting ray,
dolphins feeding far away, never sleeping.

This is the place of constant vigil,
where Madam Pele and Shark God, Akua Mano
make love in the deep.
She, hot passion: he, cool wisdom.
They own this place of knowing where I am a visitor.

Where the earth's shelf slides over magma fissure,
melted stones pour forth, fan out, become new earth,
fire blazes to the sea.

This is Honaunau coffee land,
with mango, lychee, papaya, and *ʻulu*.

The earth wound from the Bay
goes all the way to Pele's mountain,
where from the sweeping curtain of fire,
Her luminous cloud-face peers down
onto the flames, lit by her own womb's glow.
No trace of anger, only a mother's tender smile
on her full Hawaiian lips,
she looks into the molten mirror,
billowing smoke for hair
and sees her image floating there.

No slave of time, some day
she will reach all the way into the bay.
Go or stay, it makes no difference anyway,
Her kingdom is forever.

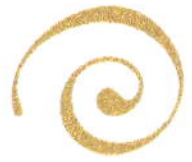

Pele's Prerogative

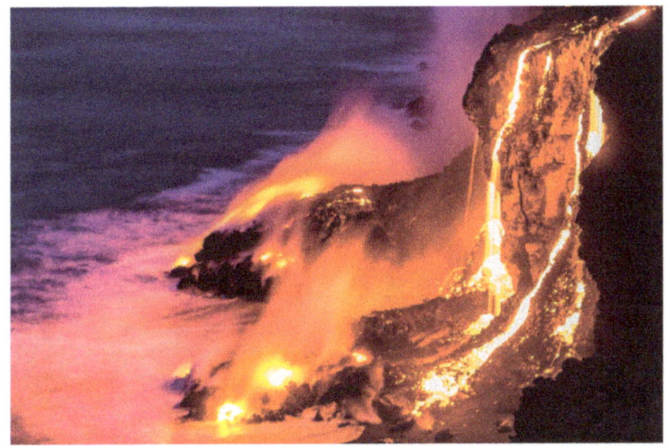

Kīlauea Volcano

Madam Pele represents
the fire inside a woman.
Her countenance encompasses
both feminine and human.

Passionate, creative,
she hurls forth new black earth,

heedless of the separateness,
between death and birth.

She comes as a young beauty,
seductive in her flow.
She comes as an old, withered crone,
her pensive movements slow.

She comes a jealous lover,
possessive and possessed,
and as a hostess generous,
heaps bounty on her guests.

Prone to wild impatience,
so thoughtless and abrupt,
yet she could wait ten thousand years,
'til choosing to erupt.

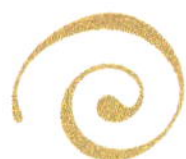

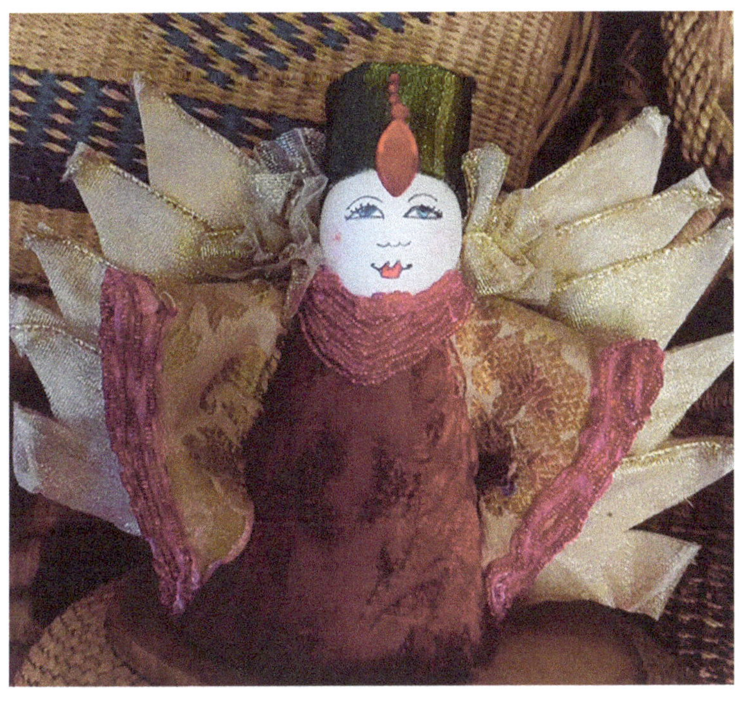

Final Reflections

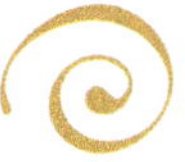

Advocate

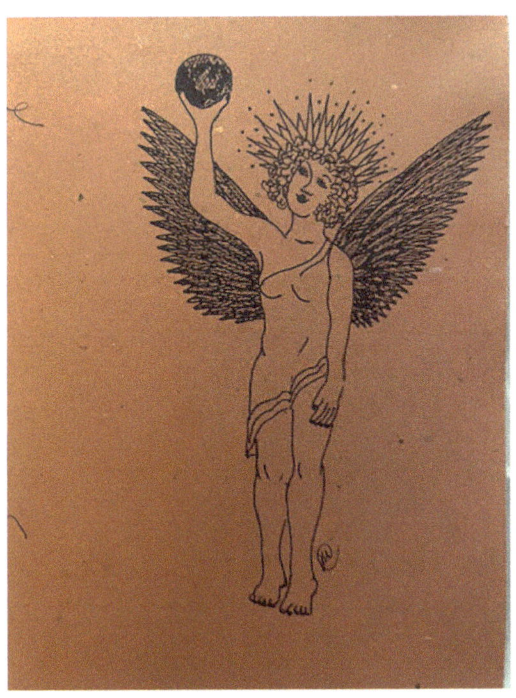

Angel with the World

I was stacking up my hurts one day, like a cord of wood, remembering the wounded, abused, misunderstood.

I built the tower of Babel, an Egyptian pyramid,
of all the indignation, the cruelties you did.

I carved the walls with rococo—gargoyles everywhere,
to keep the child molesters and killers out of there.

I laid a thousand flowers around the castle wall,
remembering each story, betrayals before the fall.

I've decorated everything, the tombstones and trees,
to honor every victim, brought onto their knees.

The ones who prayed for mercy, kneeling in the dust,
asking for compassion until their voices rust.

I decided to speak for them, the innocent and mute.
I will be the advocate, charge, and substitute.

I'll be your great-godparent, champion, and choice.
Trust me with your troubles, I will be your voice.

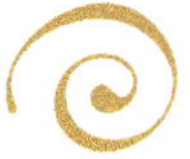

Dear Dad, 1967

Dear Dad,

It must be hurtful that I haven't written to you and called so infrequently. My intention is not to hurt you. There might be little chance of enjoying the intimate and warm relationship I had with Mom, but I want to make an attempt. I want to reach out, give you an idea of my perspective, and yes, my pain regarding my relationship with you.

I doubt you have any idea what my burden looks like. My original pain stems from the molestation by Grampa through my childhood and especially when we lived in Texas. I am hurt that you couldn't protect me from him. I know it is unreasonable to wish for that since you were unaware it was happening and since it is long past. I don't blame you that it happened. But it does seem reasonable that you would express to me your sorrow that I was abused and raped by him. It has informed my adult life, my relationship to men, and my self-esteem. I have had to work hard to make peace with the fact of it. You have yet to mention it to me, no remorse, regret, or offering of comfort for the suffering that has been inflicted on me. You did once refer to Grampa as a child molester in a letter. This brought me no comfort but did make me aware that you at least acknowledge it did in fact happen.

I'm sure it was what you learned from your mother and thought it best, but it hurts that you used your belt on me.

It hurts me that I didn't receive the attention I so craved from you when I was a child. The only time I remember you holding me was when my feet were burned so badly by running through a campfire. You ran, carrying me to the car to take me to the doctor. All these years, I tenderly remember you cradling me.

It hurts me that every conversation, every correspondence, is marked by pushing your religion on me, preaching to me. You have shown no interest in my spiritual beliefs, that they might be valid, or at least bring me comfort and refuge. There seems to be no room for that. My evaluation of the worth of a person does not hinge on them being a good Christian but being a good person.

I am a good person, Dad. I work hard, show compassion to others, pursue and cultivate the gifts God has given me. I care deeply about humanity and this world. All my life, I have been a seeker, praying daily to know God's will for me and for the power to carry that out.

What's passed is past. I love you and know you love me. It pains me though, to not have a true connection with you, to feel in our conversation your interest in my life, your concerns for my worries and troubles. I have to interrupt you to say something about myself. It makes it hard for me.

Please know this letter is not an attempt to blame and chastise you. I have no interest in angering or disrespecting you. I know you did your very best. You were a loyal husband, a good breadwinner, provider of food, clothing, hearth and home. You went out of your way to take us on adventures, vacations, boat rides, caroling trips, you brought fun and humor into my life. I am grateful for you, and I love you so dearly. I am hoping this letter will help me to bridge the gap and provide an opening to feeling truly connected and respected by you.

Love always and forever,
your #1 daughter, Jane

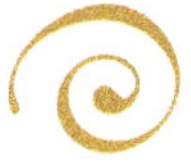

Forgiveness

Forgiveness leaves a flower-strewn
footpath in its wake,
and the fragrances of innocence,
incense, and chocolate cake.

The footpath leads to higher ground,
where the air is clear and sweet,
with the softest grass upon it,
you can tread there in bare feet.

The view from the top so expansive,
you can see the curve of the earth,
over the edge of infinity,
where the sun and moon take birth.

You can see the ocean sparkle,
the graceful seabirds fly,
panorama so breathtaking,
it could almost make you cry.

From the jutting mountain snowcaps
to the dusty desert floor,

the teeming steamy jungles,
the tropical island shore.

Forgiveness finds its way from there,
to where it found its start,
within the subtle mystery
of the noble human heart.

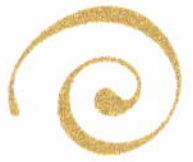

Incest Survivors

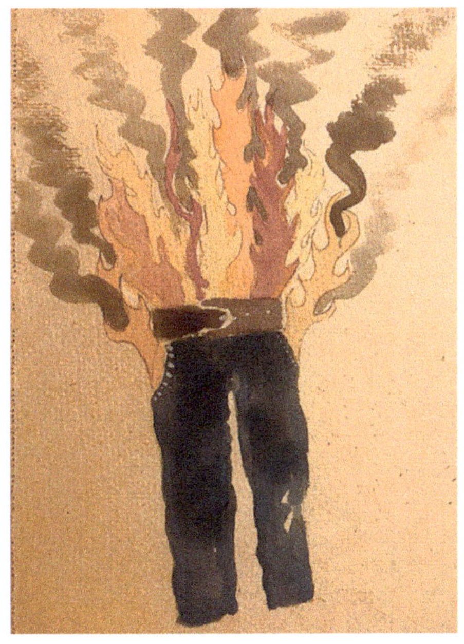

Pants on Fire

Incest survivors, history revivers,
heal the wounds down to the quick.
Don't pass along the crippling stick,
it festers and will make you sick.

Remember what you know.

Turn your face up to the light,
use it in your noble fight.
Find your peace, make it right.
Love deeply, you will grow.

Let the castle fall apart,
the frozen moat, the broken heart.
Light the flame, it's safe to start
keening to the moon.

Leave the fallout where it lies.
Take the mirror, see your eyes,
no veils or shrouds, and no more lies.
The past goes in the tomb.

Trust again that innocence,
with possibilities immense.
Show interest in the present tense,
love will find you soon.

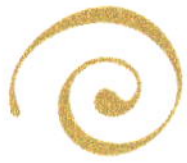

Kate

How many times have you caught me mid-air?
How many times have you taught me you're there?

Kate sleeps in sweetness,
soft groans and gentle snoring
punctuate her dreams,
which I cannot know
until she tells me,
and she will.

Her warmth fills the whole room,
even though
she is neatly
on her own side
of the bed.

The affection I feel for her
is so tender
it makes me weep.
She is the closest
relative to kindness.

When she wakes,
I'll describe to her
the sunrise.

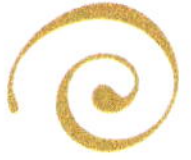

San Jacinto Sunrise

Here the morning sun is born
to the proud Mount San Jacinto,
dressed in pink and mauve,
wearing a shawl of luminescent clouds.
This sun touches the little desert fox,
the flying shadow, black crow.
The warm breath of this newborn sun
melts the clouds that were solid,
then gauzy chiffon, then gone.
This young sun now embraces
the lacy, grey-green tamarind,
the sentinel palms.
The desert floor receives the golden light,
revealing the shadow patterns
of cactus creosote and sage.
This joyful pulsing messenger,
sends long shadows along the sand,
gives the birds their bearings,
warms the wind that is the only sound.
To hail the one sun,
who is now stretching arms

across the whole desert,
marking every corner with hope,
every fold in the mountain,
every wrinkle in my brain,
the birth now complete.

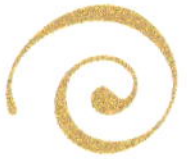

Time on a Tightrope

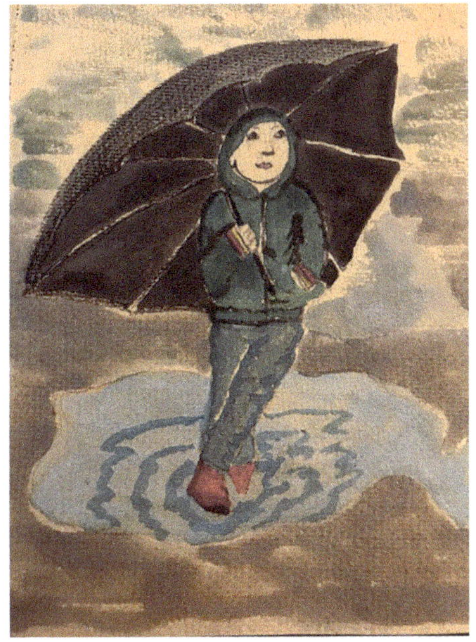

Ronan with Umbrella

A toddler chasing shallow tides
is suddenly a man.
A crone tends the child at play,
a young mother yesterday.

Spring flowers, vibrant grow,
tomorrow buried in the snow.
Winter waits for summer, then
blink, it's winter once again.

Fools attempt to still the waves,
hold on to the sun.
Time unfolds her leafy wings,
and flies for everyone.

A thin divide separates,
future tense from past.
Dare to walk this tightrope,
unbound by time, at last.

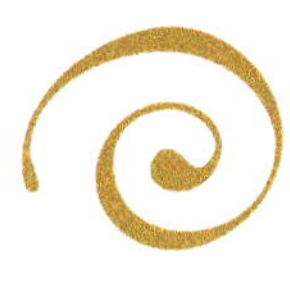

Acknowledgements

It takes a village certainly applies to this effort. I consider myself a friend millionaire as I am blessed with so many dear friends.

First, let me acknowledge my sister, Lynn Marie "Babe" Helvey, who loves me even when I don't love myself.

A nod to my East Coast girlfriends, Susanna Brackman and Claudia Stroud. These women have offered me consistent support over the years and particularly on this project.

And to my Big Island women who give me endless *Aloha*: Christine Thomas, Amy Boyd Loratta, Joan Gannon, and Monica Harwood. *Mahalo* for your *kōkua*.

Tip of the hat to my caring and sharing Pacific Palisades Women's Group for keeping me sober and somewhat sane.

Thank you, Kate Arnesen for being the soul of loving kindness. Thank you, Cathy Reback for your loyalty and wisdom. Thank you, Tracy Mestrez for your unconditional love and comic relief. And I'm grateful for my buddy Ashley Wrobel who always has my back.

A special acknowledgment to my editor Martha Fuller who remained patient throughout the process of shaping and assembling this collection—putting one foot in front of the other, even when I was spinning out of control.

And I want to humbly thank the generous donors who've kept the *Jane's World* ship afloat: Lyle Poncher, David Simons, Susanna Brackman, Mary Ellen Klee, Claudia Stroud, Amy Boyd Loratta, Lee Cone, Martha Crawford, Les Vogel, Samantha Lyons, and finally, my dear friend Lily Dulan, without whom this book would never have seen the light of day.

About the Author

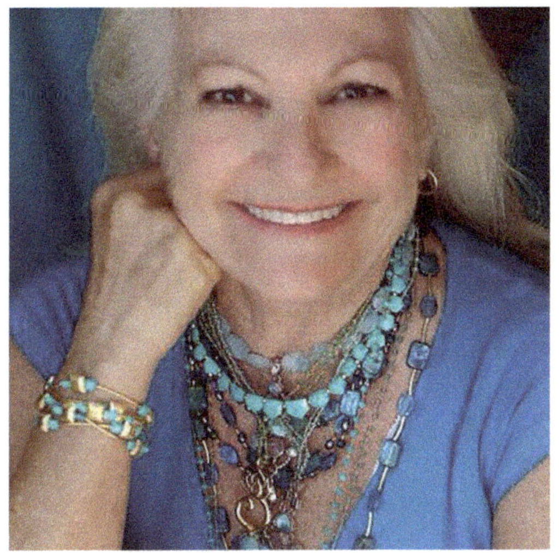

Jane Watkins

Jane is a seeker, whose journey has led her from Big Sur to New York City, India, Hawaii and beyond. At Esalen she studied with Fritz Pearls, and in Arica, Chile, she studied with Oscar Ichazo.

"I've been looking for God until I realized that God is not lost. The ocean is my church and compassion is my practice, still working on the lifetime endeavor of self-compassion."

She is an artist, yogi, and a dancer trained in African dance at the African Cultural Center in Harlem, New York by Baba Olatunji. Her art creations include drawings, paintings, ceramics, batik, tie-dye, and jewelry.

Jane enjoys thirty-eight years of continuous sobriety, "a study and a gift in itself." She lives in Santa Monica, a scant eight blocks from the ocean (her church). She lives with her roommate, Deborah Salt, and until very recently, her eighteen-year-old kitty, Honu, who died on December 1, 2025. *Jane's World* is her first book.

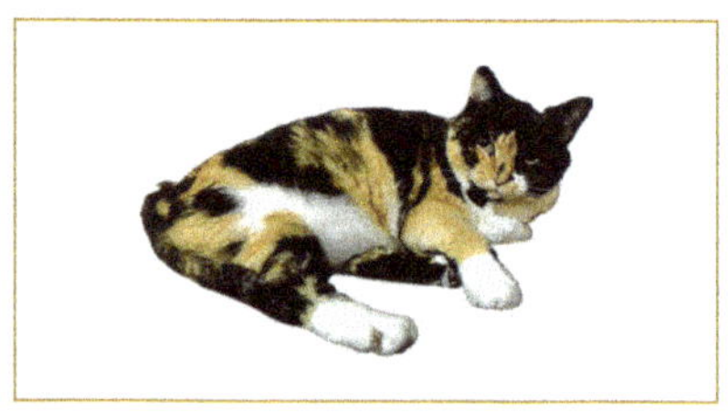

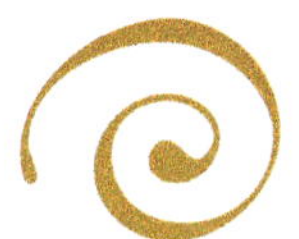

This book is typeset in Museo, a contemporary semi-serif typeface and Cochin a serif face. Display type is Marydale, a handlettering font. Cover type is Goucester MT Extra Condensed.